Learn Bearmaking

Acknowledgments

When I met Robbie Fanning, my publisher, she asked whether I considered myself a designer or a writer. I answered, "Designer." But her question pinpoints why there are few good books on making wonderful works of art, like teddy bears. In books written by writers, the designs are uninspired. In books written by designers, the directions are often confusing and abstract.

My goal is to balance these extremes. Luckily, Robbie, a *writer* (high praise from an aspiring one), strengthened my weak side. She cut no corners. Loving my book from the start, she helped me learn writing so that I could convince *you* to Learn Bearmaking.

Robbie's team nurtured and enriched the book. Lee Phillips turned her photography studio into a teddy bear wonderland for two days, complete with glitter, snowflakes, and bubbles. Larry Brazil patiently photographed tools and bear faces. Pam Poole and Martha Vercoutere smoothed out my rough sketches and made sense of each page. Tony Fanning cleaned up after all of us. I thank them for their expertise, their precision, and their patience.

Others bolstered me, too. Teddy bear artists and friends listened as I bounced ideas. My students tested new patterns, making suggestions, pointing out improvements. Teddy bear collectors, especially those who have taken my bears into their homes and hearts, sent enthusiastic letters of support.

My family was there for me, too. To my dad, who edited the first draft; to my mom, who encouraged with pride; to my mother-in-law and sister, who cross stitched models; to my husband, Joe, and daughter, Laura, who took my obsession in stride—I say, "Thank you for believing."

Learn Bearmaking

Easy • Intermediate • Advanced

by Judi Maddigan

Chilton Book Company, Radnor, PA

Copyright © 1989 by Judi Maddigan

Published in Radnor, Pennsylvania, by Chilton Book Company

Library of Congress Catalog Card Number 88-063279

ISBN 0-932086-12-8 hardbound

ISBN 0-932086-13-6 softbound

Designed by Martha Vercoutere

Illustrations by Pamela S. Poole

Color photos © Lee Phillips

B&W photos © Larry Brazil

Pattern illustrations by Lee G. Showalter

Computer aid by Tony Fanning

Singer sewing machine courtesy of Douglas Fabrics, Palo Alto, CA

Hand model: Laura Maddigan

Cross stitched models by Barbara Maddigan & Joan Harrison

Proofreading by Ben Bogdan

Bearly Adequate™ and Chubby Cubby™ are trademarked by Judi Maddigan

3 4 5 6 7 8 9 0   2 1 0 9 8 7 6 5

Contents

Foreword

When Judi Maddigan approached me with her teddy bear book, I was not familiar with the strange effect making bears has on a person. Having sewn for years, I had made a few stuffed items, but I don't think of myself as someone who sews toys or dolls—yet when I look back, there have been a continuing series of memorable ones.

It began 19 years ago when, as a gift for a nephew, I made "Roarmore," a stuffed lion from a woman's magazine. He had a fake-fur body and a rug-yarn mane. Somehow, my husband, Tony, got caught up in the making and soon Roarmore had a hand-made cage. I liked sewing and stuffing Roarmore because it was fast and easy. But it was when I began to embroider his face that something strange happened. I can't explain the feeling. One minute Roarmore was merely a pleasant diversion; the next he was much more. When his eyes took shape, I fell in love with him.

Soon our daughter came along. With a name like Kali Koala, her stuffed animal needs were amply met by relatives. I sewed only a few toys.

The next memorable incident came the summer before seventh grade. Kali was going to a two-week summer camp for the first time. She was also starting to sew a lot and had bought many patterns, including a stuffed jester. I had made her purple pindot pajamas for camp. She decided the jester, too, should be made of purple pindot, that it should accompany her to camp, and that I

should make it. Naturally, she decided this the night before. I thought, "It's not like tailoring a jacket; how hard can it be?" and stayed up to sew.

Once again, a strange thing happened when it came time to glue on the felt for the face. There I was, near midnight, a perfectly ordinary home sewer working on cloth and clothespins...and poof! as in Pinocchio, a fairy godmother touched my jester with her magic wand: he came alive. My daughter took the jester to camp that summer and today he sits on top of her bookcase.

Her relationship with the jester, though, is strange: she doesn't play with him, look at him, or even dust him. Yet she has declared that if the jester or a single one of her koala bears, dolls, or toys "disappears" (the family euphemism for donations to Goodwill) when she goes to college, she'll take away all my sewing machines when I'm not looking. "My dolls and animals are part of my childhood," she declares with 17-year-old worldliness, "and someday I may want to recapture my childhood. Besides, I like them."

The latest chapter in the toy/doll saga is the teddy bear I recently made from Judi's pattern. I made Wispy (Chapter 5) for a friend's new baby and it took only three evening classes with Judi and some outside hours of pinning, sewing, and stuffing. New for me was using snap-in nose and eyes and forming the mouth by sculpting the muzzle with invisible stitches.

New also was the rabid subcult I had innocently entered. These people *love* teddy bears, though only half of the subcult loves to make them. The other half collects them, paying $150 and up for artist teddy bears. (The world record is $86,350 for a 1920 German Steiff Teddy sold at Sotheby's.) They have teddy bear magazines and conventions and sales and stores.

As we worked in class, I asked others why they made bears. "It's fast and it's easy and it doesn't involve fitting," said one. "I began after my mother died," said another, "and it helped me work through my grief." "It's a special gift for each of my grandchildren," said another.

Tony and Kali hung over me as I worked on Wispy. They began to argue about whose bear it would be, his or hers. "Oh no," I said. "This is for Gail's baby." The arms and legs filled, the belly plumped, the face took shape—and again, I was in love. Meanwhile Tony and Kali staged mock wars over the bear, one or the other absconding to a far part with the bear. One night I found Tony asleep on the couch during Monday night football, his arms embracing Wispy.

I finished Wispy but neither of them would let me send it to the baby. I had to buy more fur and supplies and now I have to make not one, but two more bears. It's strange.

Robbie Fanning, Publisher

Note: Parts of this appeared in Robbie's column in "Needlecraft for Today" and is reprinted with permission.

Preface

A television program changed my life. It featured a skindiver who worked for an aquarium. That young woman loved her underwater world. In the interview, she said how lucky she felt to work at the one job she wanted to do most in her life.

There is no way I'd voluntarily dive into a tank of huge fish, but her enthusiasm lured me. What exactly did I want to do? What did I want to accomplish? What gave me the most enjoyment?

Since you're holding my bearmaking book, you might assume my answer was, "Make

teddy bears," but I hadn't discovered them yet. At that time, I worked for a computer firm in Silicon Valley. I decided to quit my 8:00 to 5:00 job and to do what I had wanted since college: design sewing projects for magazines.

One of my early projects was a teddy bear. When I set the eyes in that first teddy, I was stunned. This was no longer just a pile of fabric and stuff. This was a little being with feelings, needs, and sympathetic understanding behind those intelligent eyes. Against bait like that, I didn't stand a chance. I fell hook, line and sinker—and have been making bears ever since.

Fish and teddy bears. You might not think they have much in common. To that TV skindiver, those fish were her companions, her playmates,

her friends, and her reason to work every day. For me, teddy bears hold the same fascination.

But the attraction to teddy bears is not the bears alone. It's people. In the business world, I felt many employees put on a facade and related to each other on superficial levels. Everyone I've met through teddy bears has been honest, straightforward, and enthusiastic. Hand someone a teddy bear and he or she instantly becomes warm and friendly and approachable. And if the bear you offer is a gift you've made yourself, you win a feeling of satisfaction and pride that's hard to match.

Each handmade bear is an individual, and when you make one, you'll understand what I mean. Although you may use my patterns, your bear will reflect *your* personality. His expression will mirror *your* thoughts.

This is what I want to share with you in this book. This is what I want you to discover. Hold my hand and jump in feet first. Submerge yourself in my world—the teddy bear world.

Judi Maddigan
San Jose, CA

1. Bear Beginnings

Introduction

If you know how to sew, I want to teach you to make teddy bears—even if you've never worked with fur fabric or stuffed animals. Give me your attention for a few hours, and in return, I'll introduce you to a whole new world.

The teddy bear world always holds a few surprises. First you'll discover that bearmaking differs from garment sewing, although both require similar skills. And once you start a bear, it won't take you long to realize you're not working on an inanimate object.

You see, there is a moment when every teddy bear comes alive. The magic usually happens when you work on the face and creating that face is a remarkable process. Everyone who can sew can do it. There is no right or wrong way to capture an expression, and no bears are failures. Each is precious and lovable because of his individuality.

This is confirmed for me every time I teach others to make teddy bears, especially people who have never sewn a bear before. Something extraordinary happens when someone creates his or her first bear, and I love to watch it happen.

Let me paint a picture of a typical class. It will give you an idea of what to expect when you make your first bear. First, the students and I tackle the preliminaries—cutting out the pieces, sewing them together, and starting to stuff. In the beginning, you can feel the nervousness in the room. But as we progress, a great sense of anticipation replaces it. Marvelous shapes begin to emerge. One person stuffs firmly; another stuffs light. Some bears sit up in their own perky way; others are soft and cuddlesome. One bear cocks his head to the side inquisitively, while another looks up impatiently, waiting for his mouth to be stitched.

By now, the class is no longer a group of strangers. Everyone watches the bears taking shape, each one developing his or her own personality, each remarkably different, even though all use identical patterns.

Then we soft-sculpt the faces. You can't imagine the excitement until you do it yourself. The bears suddenly awaken. Their eyes twinkle, or plead to be picked up. Their mouths turn up at the corners, happy, content, or sassy.

Confidence blossoms. Each student has produced something unique. They all know they have done a wonderful job because their bears are constructed expertly and will not fall apart. They can't wait for their families and friends to meet these little beings they have created. And they make plans to sew more bears. Many more bears. One for Jason, one for Aunt Susan...the lists go on. No other gift means as much as one you make your-

self, and here is a gift they can give with pride.

Teaching others to make bears is as rewarding to me as making my own. I find the same sense of accomplishment and wonder in both activities. In this book, I hope to convey to you how much I love the *process* of bearmaking. I have an aversion to assembly lines and make my bears one by one. I enjoy shopping for fur, cutting it out, machine stitching, jointing, stuffing, hand sewing, soft-sculpting, tinting the pile...there's not one step I dislike.

This book will explain that process, so that you, too, will enjoy bearmaking. Here's how the book is organized. Chapter 2 discusses the basics: supplies, fur fabrics, and pattern templates. The rest of the text is divided into three parts: Beginning, Intermediate, and Advanced. Each part has three chapters—a technique chapter that builds on previous technique chapters, followed by two pattern chapters.

The six teddy bear patterns are presented in order of difficulty, and most have counted cross stitched accessories. (The accessories are included in the chapter with the bear they were designed for, rather than graded by skill level.) The easy patterns in Chapters 4 and 5 spell out each step in detail. The intermediate and advanced patterns assume that you have already learned some bearmaking techniques. They give concise directions (such as "pin two ear pieces together," without repeating the how-to-pin instructions found in the beginning patterns).

You do not need to read the book cover to cover before you start a bear. For example, a beginner can make one of the easy patterns after only reading Chapters 2 and 3. If you have some bearmaking experience, the techniques in Chapters 2, 3, 6, and 9 will allow you to tackle the advanced patterns.

The text does assume some basic sewing skills. Although many terms are defined in the Glossary, you'll find it easier if you have had previous experience with machine stitching (darts, easing, clipping and grading seams, etc.). However, you need no specialized background with pile fabrics or stuffed animals.

I would sum up my basic bearmaking philosophy as follows: Don't cut corners if it means compromising the quality of the finished product. Given a choice between two construction methods—one that is quick, and another that is better but takes twice the time—I invariably opt for the latter.

On the other hand, I value timesaving techniques. Note that my pattern directions are grouped differently from traditional sewing directions. When constructing a bear, I pin as much as possible at one time, and then machine sew. For example, I pin the ears, arms, legs, head, and body first, and then seam. Consequently, the pages are divided into separate columns for pinning and sewing, with step-by-step illustrations. If you prefer to handle less pieces at one time, read the directions across (rather than down) the page. Pin the ears; sew the ears; then proceed to the arms, and so on.

Some bearmakers design teddy bears specifically for adult collectors. This book, however, makes every attempt to assure the patterns are as child-safe as possible. This means avoiding the obvious hazards, like small, detachable pieces that could be swallowed, or glass eyes that could break. It also means avoiding the less-obvious hazards, like long ribbons tied around the bear's neck. (In order to be like "Teddy," some children have tied the colorful ribbons around their own necks.) And also mindful of children, the suggested fabrics and stuffing materials are durable and non-allergenic.

Even though child safety was an utmost concern, all parents should judge for themselves the appropriateness of the teddy bear (and the accessories) for their individual child. Supervise an infant or a toddler prone to put everything in his or her mouth. Don't leave him unattended, chewing on fur ears or teething on fabric-covered noses. Teddy bears, marvelous critters that they are, will wait ever so patiently upon a dresser or shelf until their owners have matured to the age of, say, three or four years.

Sometimes, after the time and effort that goes into a handmade bear, the maker doesn't want a child playing with his or her creation. Will the teddy be dragged by a paw through the sandbox, or be fed crayons, or meet some other unmentionable fate? Perhaps, but children and teddy bears were made for each other. If you have any doubt about the importance of a special teddy in a child's life, read *The Teddy Bear Book* by Peter Bull (listed in the Bibliography). He argues the case more eloquently than I.

No matter how many bears you make, each will be special. Your teddy will place no demands on you, yet will always be there when you need him. He will patiently wait with his all-knowing smile, growing wiser with the years, collecting memories, meaning more to you all the time. And when you look at him, you'll remember the comment your best friend made when she saw him for the first time, or you'll think of the holidays you and your teddy shared. You'll remember the thoughts that ran through your mind during the hours you cut and stitched. Looking at that marvelous bear, you'll think of the time and the best efforts you spent...and you'll know it was worth it.

If I had to choose only one concept to communicate through this book, it would be to share. Give someone a teddy bear. Once you've learned bearmaking, teach someone else. Share your bears with your family and friends, and let them discover the charm for themselves.

2. Bear Essentials

Fur Fabric and Supplies

Making a wonderful teddy bear starts *before* you sit down at your sewing machine to sew the first stitch. Start right by having the necessary supplies handy, selecting an appropriate pile fabric, and preparing master pattern templates.

Basic Supplies

Aside from a sewing machine and threads, discussed in Chapter 3, the following tools and supplies will ease your job (Fig. 2.1). Also check the optional tools listed in Chapter 9.

Screwdriver or other stuffing tool: Stuffing a bear with only your hands is not enough. You will need a tool, but the choice of a stuffing tool is a highly personal matter. I packed fiberfill into my early bears with the handle of a wooden spoon. (Some professional bearmakers still use this method.) Using a screwdriver improved this procedure. Screwdrivers come in many shapes and sizes to fit your hand, and their wedged tip provides directional control. I alternate between two sizes, with overall lengths of about 8" and 10". (Fig. 2.2) Screwdrivers work so well for me, I haven't given the newer, specially designed Stuffing Sticks™ a reasonable trial. Many teddy bear artists have recommended them, though, because the

handles rest comfortably across your palm, requiring less gripping strength.

3-1/2" and 5" soft sculpture dollmaking needles: Thanks to the popularity of soft sculpture dolls, these long, slender needles are readily available. (See Fig. 2.3.) You will use them for most of your hand sewing. When purchasing, study the needle tips on several cards of the same size. Choose long, gently tapering points which pull through your material easily, rather than blunt, stubby ones. Additionally, intermediate and advanced patterns require a 7" soft sculpture needle.

8" toymaker's needle (optional): This is not for sewing, but for pulling out any pile fibers trapped in the seams. A long upholstery needle (about gauge 14) may be substituted.

1/8" hole punch: Available in office supply (stationery) stores, this punch is used for the pattern templates. The 1/8" size, smaller than the more common 1/4" paper punch, offers greater precision.

Awl: An awl pokes through the material for inserting eyes,

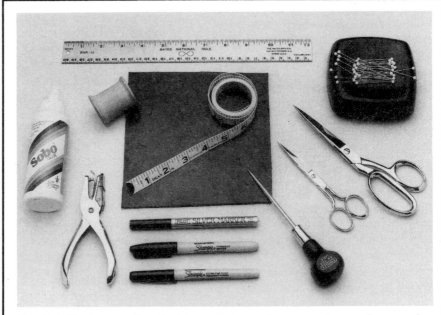

Fig. 2.1 Basic supplies for bearmaking: scissors, awl, wooden spool, rubber sheet, 1/8" hole punch, permanent marking pens and paint pen, quilting pins, tape measure, ruler, and white glue.

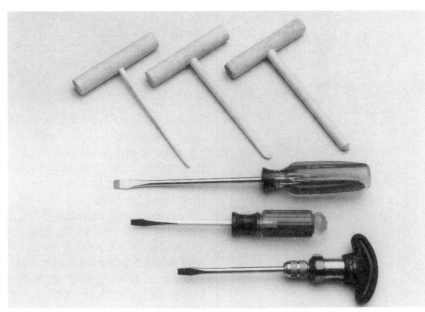

Fig. 2.2 **Making It Bearly** *designed these easy grip, hardwood Stuffing Sticks™ (above) specifically for the bearmaker. They come in a variety of sizes with a choice of three different tips (corresponding to a chopstick, a screwdriver, and a wooden spoon).*

piece measuring 6" by 6". Precut pieces of rubber about that size (for gaskets) are sold with plumbing supplies.

Scissors: You'll need shears with sharp tips for fur fabric, and regular scissors for pattern templates. (See cutting techniques in Chapter 3.) Shears with a knife edge, like those manufactured by Gingher, manage furs well. In addition, a pair of small, sharp scissors helps when trimming fur around a bear's eyes.

Fine, permanent, felt-tip black marking pen: Make sure this pen is specifically labeled "permanent." Buy a black, not a colored, one because sometimes the same manufacturer's colored pens state they are not for cloth. If you choose a dark fur, you will need an additional silver, white, or other light-colored paint pen for marking. (A paint pen has a metal barrel with a ball that mixes the paint when you shake it.)

noses, and joints. It separates the fabric threads rather than cutting holes like scissors. Don't shop in a fabric store for this item; a hardware store has awls with larger, more comfortable handles.

Wooden spool: To help install safety eyes and noses, a wooden spool fits over their shanks to tighten the washers. My favorite one measures 1-3/4" high and 1-1/2" in diameter, but size isn't critical.

Sheet rubber: To prevent scratching the eyes, pad your work surface. You can use folded fabric, but I like a piece of sheet rubber. Besides

cushioning the eyes, the rubber prevents them from slipping. Some hardware stores sell reinforced rubber sheet by the square foot, cut to size. One-quarter square foot gives you a

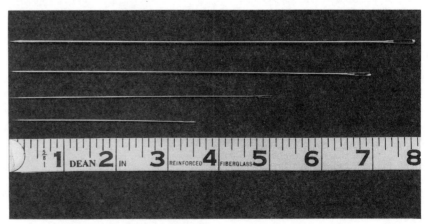

Fig. 2.3 Most hand sewing is done with soft sculpture dollmaking needles. The largest needle frees fur trapped in stitching lines.

Quilting pins: Because pile fabrics are bulky, they require larger pins than regular fabrics. Pick plastic-headed quilter's pins about 1-3/4" long.

Tape measure and ruler.

White glue: Choose a fabric glue that dries strong, clear, and flexible. An arts and crafts glue like Sobo® works well.

How To Select Fur Fabrics

The most critical aspect of teddy bear making is the choice of fur fabric. No amount of beautiful handiwork can disguise inferior materials, so let's discuss some important points you should consider before you buy.

One of the joys of bearmaking is watching your bear take shape in a quality imitation fur. The density of the fibers helps determine quality. Bend the fabric back on itself and notice how easily you can see the backing through the pile (Fig. 2.4). If the fibers are thin, the backing will be noticeable in the finished bear.

If you have a fur sample, judge the quality by distressing it. Rub the pile in a circular motion with your thumb, and then brush it smooth again. How well it recovers will forecast how the fur will stand up to playful handling. Avoid fibers that fall out, break, or remain permanently bent out of shape.

Price provides an indication of quality—and price range is enormous. A domestic fur costing five times as much as another fur from the same store should be thicker and more luxurious. Don't necessarily buy the most expensive

Fig. 2.4 When curled backwards, the left fur's backing shows. The fur on the right is superior.

Fig. 2.5 The longest fibers of this high-quality fur were damaged by winding backwards on the bolt.

fur you can find, but do recognize that a cheap fur is a false economy. Poor fabric produces an inferior bear that will deteriorate. It simply is not worth your time.

Next, consider the ways fabric shops store and display their fur. (These are good points to remember when you store your own furs at home, too.) The best method is fabric rolled on 60"-long, heavy cardboard tubes. In contrast, when furs are folded in half, lengthwise, and wound around shorter, flat cardboard (like regular yardage bolts), they develop a permanent center crease that interferes with pattern layout. Avoid flat-folded remnants on tables, with matted, crushed pile. Occasionally, steaming can restore the pile, but work conservatively, trying it on a remnant first. While steaming, brush the fur gently against the nap to raise the pile.

One more point about bolts: sometimes, furs are wound incorrectly. The nap of the fabric (the way the pile lays down) should run *toward* the raw edge (the leading, cut edge) of

Fig. 2.6 Imitation furs have either a woven backing (left) or a knit backing (right). The type of backing makes a critical difference in the finished bear's shape.

the bolt, not sideways toward the selvage. The nap should never run toward the center of the bolt because in the process of rolling, the pile fibers fold back on themselves and crush (Fig. 2.5).

Fur fabrics have either a woven or a knit backing (Fig. 2.6). A woven fabric stretches on the bias; a knit has more crosswise stretch. Each pattern in this book specifies either knit or woven fabric because the stretch will affect the shape of the stuffed pieces.

The first three patterns in this book call for *knit furs*. (Chapter 6 discusses the *woven furs* used for the last three patterns.) Knit furs usually run 58" to 60" wide and have a stabilized backing. The stiffness of the backing differs greatly. Select a pliable one because an inflexible backing jams the sewing machine and will complicate construction techniques.

Examine the backing. The rows of stitches should be packed tightly together, even and consistent across the entire width. Stretch the fabric to evaluate the crosswise stretch. It should be stable and should recover its shape. The lengthwise stretch should be barely discernible.

Next, choose the pile height. Each pattern recommends a specific pile height. A different length of pile will change the bear's appearance dramatically, which you may want. But for a bear with a predictable appearance, you should measure the pile instead of estimating by sight. See Fig. 2.7.

Now consider color. Many of the photos in this book have

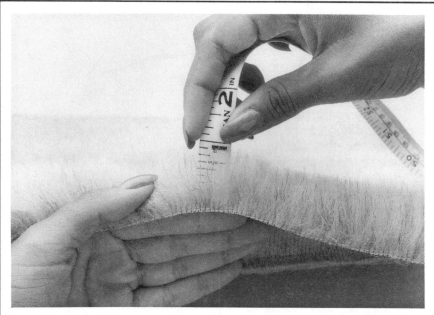

Fig. 2.7 Actually measure the pile length when selecting a fur fabric.

Fig. 2.8 Note that the lighter Bearly Adequate's features stand out, while the darker bear's expression is more subtle.

light-colored bears. Light bears photograph well, and I also favor the lighter furs because the features—the eyes, noses, mouths, and depressions in the ears—show up better (Fig. 2.8). This is significant when you depend upon a shadow under the mouth sculpting to help shape the expression. But color is largely a matter of personal choice—both my mother and mother-in-law have near-black Bearly Adequate bears, their favorites of the eleven colors I've used for that design.

Both pile height and color help indicate the sex of a teddy bear, but mostly the bear makes up his or her own mind, and you have little to do with it. See Fig. 2.9.

Lastly, the retail supply of furs is seasonal, with the best selection available in early fall. If you have trouble locating an appropriate fur, check the Appendix's list of suppliers. Delay ordering fabric by mail until seeing an actual sample (Fig. 2.10). Even the same mill will sometimes vary bolt to bolt on the "same" fabric, so, whenever possible, choose a supplier who offers a money-back guarantee.

Now that you understand density, quality, color, pile heights, and stabilized backings, my best advice is, "Trust your instincts." Perhaps you'll find a fur you dearly love, and you may even visualize a gorgeous finished teddy in it. Don't pass it up just because it doesn't measure up to one or two criteria for an *ideal* fabric. More often than not, those "finds" make magical bears.

Fig. 2.9 The Wispy on the left has a pile height that measures 3/4", lending a masculine feeling to the finished bear. The bear on the right, with a 1-1/16" pile, is 100% little girl (she's dressed on the cover). But pile height does not necessarily determine gender. Many of my students have made their own Wispy in the same 1-1/16" fur and their bears turned out definitely male. In the case of my two Wispies, however, pile height was a prime factor.

Fig. 2.10 Some mail-order suppliers send samples of their fur fabrics for a modest fee. Check the Suppliers' list for addresses.

Pattern Templates

Once you've chosen an appealing fur, you need to transfer the pattern pieces from the book to the wrongside of your fabric. Possibilities include tracing paper (quick, but hard to handle on bulky fabric) and felt (it sticks to knit fur backings without pins, letting you cut around the pieces without marking them first). My favorite two methods involve card stock and quilter's templates (Fig. 2.11).

The first option, and hands-down easiest solution, is to photocopy the pattern from this book. (My understanding publisher permits this copyright exemption as long as the photocopies are for your personal use.) Be certain that the photocopy machine you use does not distort or shrink the pattern. Compare the photocopied pattern to the original before you copy all your patterns. If the patterns match, photocopy the pieces directly onto 8-1/2" by 11" card stock (also called "cover" weight). This heavy paper is similar to the thickness of index cards and comes in different colors. Most print shops handle the heavier paper for a nominal cost per page. If you're making more than one pattern, organize your patterns by copying each bear onto a different colored paper.

The stiff card stock pattern pieces hold their shapes while you trace around them. If desired, reinforce them with

Fig. 2.11 Make pattern masters by photocopying from the book onto cover weight paper (above), or place quilter's template plastic on the book and trace with an indelible marker.

clear self-adhesive plastic (Fig. 2.12). Store the templates in Ziploc® bags or 9" x 12" clasp envelopes.

In some cases (Wispy's Body Front and Body Back, for example), large patterns need piecing because they don't fit on one page. When cutting out the larger section of a piece that needs joining, leave about 1/4" extra paper along the line that says, "Join pattern here."

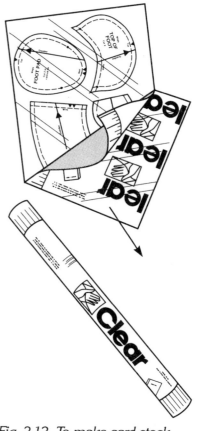

Fig. 2.12 To make card stock templates more durable, cover the full-paged photocopies with clear, self-adhesive plastic (such as Con-Tact®) before cutting them out.

Cut out the smaller section normally; then overlap the excess paper. On both the front and back, tape the two sections together along the labeled line.

After cutting out the photocopied patterns, punch holes with a 1/8" hole punch wherever dots appear on the pieces. Also punch holes for the eye placement. If you lack a hole punch, or if your punch won't reach specific dots, carefully puncture the templates with an awl.

Transfer the grainline arrows to each photocopied template's reverse side by marking the top and bottom of the arrows on the back. With a ruler, draw a line from one edge of the template to the other. Because you never actually fold the fur, you will need to flip the photocopied patterns for the shaded portions of the pattern layouts. The arrows on the reverse will help you align the grain.

The second suggestion for master patterns is quilter's templates, a longer-wearing solution. Quilting shops stock large sheets of this lightweight, transparent plastic. Place it on the book's page and trace the pattern, using a permanent marker. Trace all the markings, including full grainlines. You don't need to transfer the grainlines to the back of the templates (as with photocopies) because you can see through the plastic.

Quilter's templates also have an advantage over photocopies when a pattern says, "Place on fold." As you will read in the next chapter, you never fold the fur. Therefore, you will need to make full-sized patterns. In that instance, trace the cutting lines for one half of the piece. Make a 1/4" mark at the top and bottom of the fold line (don't draw the entire fold line) and then flip the template over. Line up the "fold" line and trace the other half of the piece. See Fig. 2.13. The 1/4" marks you made on the fold line indicate the center of the piece.

Similarly, for pieces that extend beyond one page, you can trace one section of the piece, butt the next portion, and resume drawing it as one continuous piece. Unlike photocopies, you don't need to overlap and tape the pieces together.

Cut quilter's templates with regular scissors, and punch holes for the pattern dots with a 1/8" hole punch. To mark the eye placement, or any dots your hole punch can't reach, drill with a 1/8" bit against a wood backup.

For both the quilter's templates and the photocopied card stock, clip out the solid notches along the edges of the

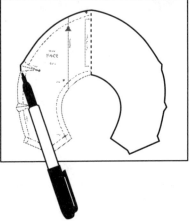

Fig. 2.13 When making quilter's templates, if a pattern says, "Place on fold," trace one half; flip the template over and trace the mirror image for the other half of the piece.

templates. This permits marking the notches on your fur without lifting the templates. You *mark* the notches, but you *cut* your fur on the solid cutting line.

Now that you've learned about supplies, fur, and master templates, I can bearly wait to show you some beginning techniques.

3. Get Your Bearings

Beginning Techniques

In Chapters 3, 4, and 5, we'll cover the bearmaking basics. You will learn all the techniques needed to sew either of the two easy patterns: Fidget, a playful hand puppet, or a non-jointed, cuddly 20" bear named Wispy.

Sure, you're eager to start your bear. But take time to read through the directions *before* you start. Include any technique chapters, like this one and Chapter 2, that precede your chosen pattern. Become familiar with the instructions, and you'll know where you're headed.

Each pattern has a separate list of materials and an individual guide for selecting an appropriate fur. Once you've chosen your pattern and have your fur and materials on hand, make a set of master pattern pieces as directed in Chapter 2. Now you're ready to trace the pieces to the back of the fur fabric.

Layout Pointers

As with garment sewing, don't toss your pattern pieces down helter-skelter and start cutting. First consider this list of seven pattern layout tips.

Tip #1: Check the rightside. Although you will copy your patterns to the wrongside of the fabric, always examine the rightside first. Check for creased, matted pile or imperfections. Mark any problems with safety pins on the wrongside of your yardage. Pay particular attention to the area for the face piece because while the body pieces can tolerate fold lines or other marks, the main face piece should be perfect.

Tip #2: Avoid the edges. The last chapter discussed the stabilized backing on knit furs. Sometimes this sizing does not extend all the way to the selvages. Do not place your pieces too close to the lengthwise edges if the selvages don't have stabilizer.

Also watch the crosswise edges. When you purchase fur, it is either cut or torn from the bolt. If cut incorrectly, the pile will be shortened along the edge. If torn, a knit fur stretches along the crosswise edge.

Tip #3: Align the grainline arrows. In your early sewing lessons, did you learn about corduroy and its "nap"? Fur fabrics also have a nap, and the direction of that nap makes a critical difference. Nowhere is the nap more apparent than on the bear's face. If the nap runs the wrong way, grumpy, frowning bears will result.

Determine the nap by rubbing your hand across the fur. *With* the nap, the pile will lay down smoothly; *against* the nap, the fibers will stand up. The pattern's lengthwise arrow shows the nap direction. Place the fur wrongside up on your cutting surface, *with the pile laying toward you*. Place the master pattern pieces *with their directional arrows pointing toward you*.

Align all grainline arrows with the stitches on the back of knit fabric. You can probably do this by sight. Don't try to measure from knit fur selvages to the marked grainlines because knit furs do not always have selvages parallel to the rows of stitches. On the other hand, woven furs do have true selvages, and for the later patterns in the book you may either measure from the selvages or align the grainlines by sight.

Tip #4: Transfer all pattern markings. Trace around the templates on the wrongside of your material, using a black, permanent marking pen. For dark furs, substitute a light paint pen. Transfer all the pattern markings—dots and notches. (Don't copy the grainlines.) Make only small marks at the dots so they don't show on the rightside of your fur. This is especially important on light-colored furs.

Some beginners find it helpful to label the body parts on the back as they cut out. Don't write directly on the fur backing; it may bleed through on light-colored furs. Instead, label a piece of masking tape and stick it temporarily onto the back of each body part.

Tip #5: Never fold fur fabric. Always work on a single layer of fabric. If a photocopied pattern templates says, "Place on fold," trace the cutting lines for one half of the piece. Make a 1/4" mark at the top and bottom of the fold line (don't draw the entire fold line) and then flip the template over. Line up the "fold" line and trace the other half. The 1/4" marks indicate the center.

Tip #6: Reverse the piece when cutting two or four. If a pattern says, "Cut 2," cut once with the template rightside up and once with the template flipped over. Always keep the directional arrows consistent, even if the pattern piece is wrongside up. Similarly, when cutting four of the same piece, cut two rightside up and two reversed. Shaded pieces on the layout diagrams correspond to reversed templates.

Tip #7: Change layouts when appropriate. Each pattern has its own layout diagram, but there's nothing magical about it. Rearrange pieces to avoid imperfections marked with safety pins, or to utilize your yardage more efficiently. Keep the nap arrows consistent.

Cutting Techniques

Before you begin to cut, be sure you are wearing old clothes and are in an appropriate room. The fur fibers tend to float all over.

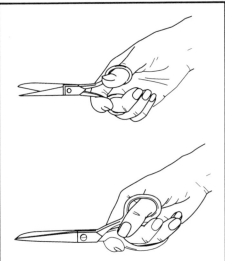

Fig. 3.1 For greater control when cutting, wrap your index finger around the handle of the scissors above the hole for your other finger(s).

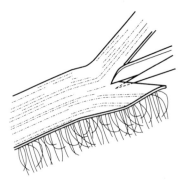

Fig. 3.2 Cut fur fabric from the wrongside, snipping through the backing. Try not to cut the pile.

Cut a single layer of fabric at a time, from the wrongside, inserting the point of your shears into the pile to part it on the cutting line. Check Figs. 3.1 and 3.2. Make small snips with the tips of the scissors, cutting only the fabric backing, not the pile. Do not clip into the seam allowances at the notches.

Dull or poor quality scissors make cutting a drudgery. If your shears need sharpening, see page 103.

Save some fur scraps. You'll find them useful for adjusting your sewing machine and for practicing new techniques. Finally, shake all the pieces outdoors, to free them of loose fibers clinging to the edges.

Pinning

Fur piles, especially long ones, will hide a multitude of minor stitching errors. One thing they won't hide, however, is fur caught in the seam lines.

You can prevent trapped pile with the right pinning method. Pin fur pieces rightsides together, *tucking all pile to the inside.* This is easy when the nap runs away from the stitching line. It's more difficult when the nap runs toward the seam allowance, so that is usually where I start pinning. (The grainline arrows point to this edge.) Place the pins at right angles to the stitching line, as in Fig. 3.3. Notice the orientation of the pins. This is upside-down compared to garment sewing, but it helps keep track of the bottom fur.

As you stitch to each pin, check that both layers of fur are feeding into the machine evenly. Remove the pin rather than sewing over it, and proceed to the next pin. By sewing in sections like this, the edges will be lined up at the end of your seam.

Machine Stitching

Before stitching, clean out the lint in your machine and oil it. Your machine cannot sew evenly unless it is properly adjusted. To fine-tune the stitching, experiment with a few sample seams on fur scraps, checking thread, needle point, and stitch quality before you tackle your bear.

Threads

For hand stitching, I like a heavy-duty nylon (#69) upholstery thread. Some fabric shops stock it in their drapery section rather than with their regular spools of thread. This nylon thread is approximately the weight of button and carpet, but may be unmanageable in many home sewing machines.

Shops specializing in industrial sewing machines sell this heavy-duty nylon thread on large cones. They also stock a slightly lighter-weight nylon thread on cones (B-46), and that's what I use for my machine stitching. This thread is between the thicknesses of regular thread and the heavy button and carpet thread. Unfortunately, it is not readily available on smaller spools, the huge cones are expensive (but they do seem to last forever), and color selection is limited.

As a substitute, consider trying *hand quilting thread* in your machine. This thread is very strong (the threads of the material will pop before seams stitched in quilting thread give way). I've also found my machine handles it easily.

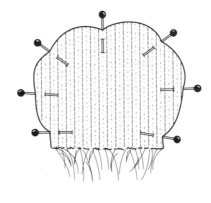

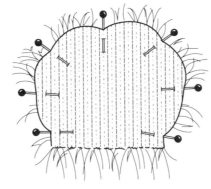

Fig. 3.3 The ears on the bottom were pinned incorrectly. Notice the pile slips out between the edges. On the top, all the pile has been tucked to the inside.

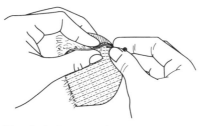

Fig. 3.4 As you place pins perpendicular to the stitching line, poke the fur toward the middle of the piece. For an ear, begin at the center top and work toward the bottom.

Luckily, the choice of machine needle is easier than the choice of thread. Depending on the thickness of your thread, select either a size 14(90) or 16(100) needle. For knit fabrics, use a ball-point needle.

Seams

Stuffing a bear firmly causes a great deal of force on the seams. As if that weren't enough, toddlers tend to dangle a teddy by one arm. Bears don't mind trailing behind their owners in this fashion, as long as their seams don't pop.

To compensate for these stresses, use a slight zigzag stitch rather than a straight machine stitch. You don't want a wide zigzag—just a hint of one will provide a little stretch to the stitching. Set the stitch width very small, and the stitch length at about 12 stitches per inch.

Some teddy bear makers use regular weight, cotton-covered polyester thread and stitch their seams twice. Newer machines have reinforced or stretch stitches that serve the same purpose. For example, they stitch forward several stitches, automatically reverse a couple of stitches, and then stitch forward again.

For an alternative, use two threads in both the needle and the bobbin. Wind the bobbin from two spools at once, treating the two strands as one thread. Thread the machine with two spools, using a separate tension disk for each, but threading both through one needle. This provides a doubled thread on both the top and bottom.

Quicker than either option is to use a heavy-duty thread if your machine will handle it.

Machine Adjustments

After adjusting your thread tensions (Fig. 3.5), notice how your fur feeds into the machine. The most common problem is when the feed dogs pull the bottom layer of fur in faster than the top. The result: you can end up with as much as 1/2" extra top layer at the end of the seam. To cure this, *loosen* the presser-foot tension so that the feed dogs don't grab at the bottom fur.

Some machines have dual feed, which cures this problem. Others have an optional walking foot attachment that feeds the top layer while the feed dogs seize the bottom one. Different brands and models have varying success rates, but a walking foot is worth investigating.

When stitching your bear, keep the pattern pieces handy for reference. All seam allowances are 1/4"; often a presser foot is the right width for a guide. Measure a few seams to confirm they are truly 1/4" wide because a small difference in seam widths will make a big difference in your bear. Say, for instance, you're off by 1/16". That doesn't sound like much. But the body typically has four pieces. Four seams mean eight seam allowances. Those "tiny" discrepancies accumulate to a full 1/2" difference in your bear's waist measurement, and most patterns won't tolerate that much inaccuracy.

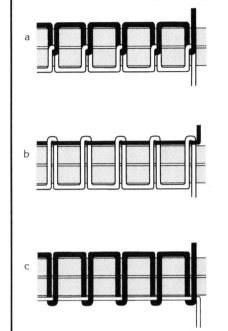

Fig. 3.5 (a) Proper tension, (b) top thread too tight, (c) bobbin tension too tight

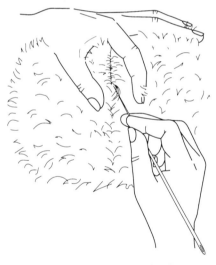

Fig. 3.6 Liberate trapped pile with the tip of a large needle.

To check the width of your presser foot, place a tape measure under the needle. Align the right side of the presser foot with any 1/4" mark. Lower the needle until it touches the tape measure. Is it exactly at the inch mark? If not, can you decenter the needle so it is exact?

This book organizes directions to allow machine sewing several bear pieces at once; just feed them in one after the other without stopping to cut the threads. Backstitch at the beginning and end of each seam to lock your threads. You may not need to lift the presser foot between some of the seams. All your pieces finish strung together on the same threads, which you later clip.

Develop the habit of checking the underside to assure a consistent 1/4" seam allowance on that layer, too. Sometimes the bottom piece shifts and the resulting seam is inconsistent.

Unless otherwise directed, before sewing over previously stitched seams, pin the seam allowances open. Never iron the seams open because the heat will crush the pile.

Trapped Pile

Despite careful pinning and stitching, when you check the rightside of the fabric you may find fur caught in the seams. To release this trapped pile, slide the tip of a large needle under it and pry the fibers up (Fig. 3.6). When I say "large needle," I mean *large*. I use a heavy, 8" needle (see the supplies list in the previous chapter) because I like the balance of the long needle in my hand. (Of all my bearmaking tools, this needle is my favorite. It executes all sorts of fussy little tasks.)

Fig. 3.7 shows an alternate tool. This wire Bunka brush raises the nap for a specialized type of Japanese embroidery. Teddy bear makers have discovered it also extricates the pile from seams. Try it on woven furs with shorter piles. For 1" knit furs, however, the Bunka brush grabs the fibers so tightly that it rips them out. We'll talk more about the Bunka brush in Chapter 9, where it becomes an indispensible aid for pile tinting. Now, on to the stuff at hand....

Stuffing Strategy

My daughter has a large manufactured teddy that started out adorably soft and huggable. Over a five-year period, the bear's stuffing shifted. His misshapen head now droops on his chest. (While my daughter still loves that bear, others might not find him irresistible.)

When people first pick up one of my teddies, they are surprised by how firmly the little guys are stuffed. Firm stuffing denotes quality in a handmade bear. It allows you to sculpt expressions that will still smile and delight in five years or fifty years. And with proper stuffing, your bears will retain their youthful figures throughout their lifetimes.

Choosing Fiberfill

My first experience with stuffing came at the age of twelve, when I sewed a mother and baby koala from a kit. The directions called for kapok. A short while into the stuffing project, with fuzzy little fibers floating about, I found I was violently allergic to kapok.

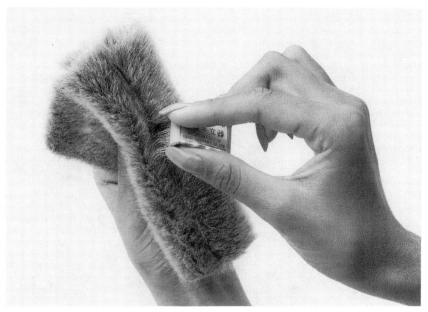

Fig. 3.7 For shorter piles, brushing the seams with a Bunka brush will lift the fibers from the stitching lines.

A good polyester fiberfill works so well for stuffing, it is foolish to waste time on any of the alternatives. It isn't lumpy, doesn't smell or attract varmints, and is non-allergenic.

Having sung the praises of 100% polyester fiberfill, I should mention a disadvantage: it takes trial and error to find the right type. It all boils down to quality and personal preference.

Price provides some indication of fiberfill quality. The "bargain" brands invariably turn out to be no bargain. Their fibers clump together. You can see little lumps when you inspect a bag of it. If you take out a handful and pull it apart, tiny fibers separate from the mass (Fig. 3.8). You would need to wear a mask to avoid breathing the fibers (Fig. 6.8), and fragments could also invade your eyes (especially irritating with contact lenses).

A top quality fiberfill has long polyester fibers that do not break into tiny, troublesome particles (Fig. 3.9). Many different brands meet this requirement, and here's where personal choice enters into it.

I won't stir up a controversy by naming specific brands because it's better for you to evaluate samples and judge them for yourself. Find a brand that handles easily and has the least tendency to lump.

Stuffing Techniques

Generally, I work with wads of stuffing as large as will conveniently fit through the opening. The body, having a larger opening than an arm, gets larger handfuls of fiberfill at one time. Pack the fiberfill into the areas furthest from the opening first. Use your screwdriver (or other stuffing tool—see Fig. 2.2) to pack each portion of fiberfill before you add more.

Fig. 3.8 If you pull apart cheap polyester fiberfill over a dark surface, you will see the tiny fibers separate. Choose a better quality.

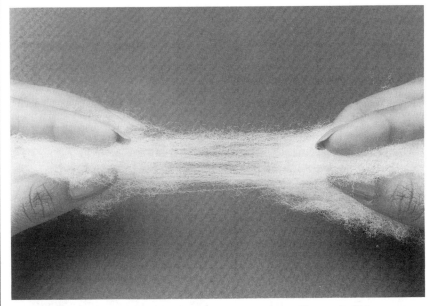

Fig. 3.9 A high-quality fiberfill has long polyester fibers. Pull it apart, and you will see few broken fragments.

Slide your fingers along the outer surface of the piece and squeeze it, checking for any bumps or other distortions. By catching problems as they happen, you can shift the stuffing and correct them.

Sometimes you will almost finish stuffing a piece, and then realize you missed a spot. Say, for example, that your bear's arm has a depression at the wrist. You can wedge additional stuffing into that area by folding some fiberfill over the tip of your screwdriver. Working through the opening, slide the screwdriver along the backing of the fur, slipping the new fiberfill between the material and the stuffing already in place. The flat tip of the screwdriver offers directional control, allowing you to maneuver the stuffing into precisely the right spot. Withdraw the screwdriver, and the added fiberfill remains in position.

Occasionally, no amount of poking and prodding will even out a shape. In those cases, take the fiberfill out, separate and fluff it, and start over.

Some bearmakers partially stuff a piece and then begin to close the opening by hand. As they stitch, they continue to add more fiberfill to the areas already closed. That way, they don't have to close an opening bulging with fiberfill. I favor finishing the stuffing first, and then stitching. This means a wad of stuffing protrudes from the opening until it is packed down and held in place by the hand sewing. Perhaps this complicates the hand work, but I prefer it to constantly handling the fiberfill while stitching. Also, you can adjust the fiberfill through the opening (as described above). Choose whichever method works best for you.

The directions for each bear give individualized stuffing instructions. They tell you when to stuff firmly, when to pack loosely, and where to cram in extra. But the secret of good stuffing technique is thinking in three dimensions.

The process of stuffing is interactive and creative, like sculpting. You have control over the shape of the pieces. How you pack the fiberfill will determine whether a paw turns in or out. As you work, turn the pieces around. View your bear from every angle because the profile is just as important as the full front view.

Hand Stitching

We've already discussed various threads for machine stitching. Hand stitching demands strong thread. Once you've stuffed the pieces, there will be substantial stresses on the stitches used to close the openings.

As mentioned a few pages earlier, a heavy-duty nylon upholstery thread (#69) is my favorite thread. If unobtainable, substitute button and carpet thread. I have snapped carpet thread when knotting, but so far have not broken the nylon. Also, nylon thread slips through the material easier and resists tangling, yet holds a knot well.

The previous chapter describes the soft sculpture dollmaking needles used for hand stitching. See Fig. 2.3.

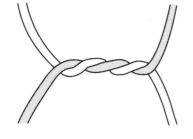

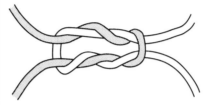

Fig. 3.10 Remember a square knot, "right over left, left over right"? Form a surgeon's square knot the same way, but intertwine the threads one extra time on both steps. Tighten the knot after tying the first half; the doubled twist prevents slipping until the second half is completed.

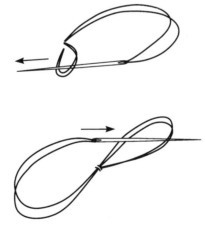

Fig. 3.11 To knot hand stitching: Take a small backstitch and bring your needle through the resulting loop. Pull on the thread at the fur surface (not on the needle) to tighten this stitch. Bring the needle through the resulting loop. Separate the two strands of thread and pull them in opposite directions to tighten the knot. If necessary, repeat.

Knots

This book assumes you have basic sewing skills. However, I will offer suggestions on knotting because you'll need more substantial knots than used for garment sewing.

First, learn a surgeon's square knot. The directions call for this knot in two instances: (1) forming a beginning knot for hand stitching, and (2) tying the bears' bows.

Fig. 3.10 illustrates how to form this knot. Although it works for both seams and soft-sculpting, knotting your sewing threads this way is optional. If you prefer another knot large enough to resist pulling through the fur fabric, feel free to use it. For tying ribbons for the bows, however, the surgeon's knot is unsurpassed because when you tighten the threads after the first step of the knot, they don't slip.

After completing the hand stitching, secure your thread as shown in Fig. 3.11 and lose the ends inside (Fig. 3.12). Each bear's directions will cover soft sculpting in detail, but the same methods for knotting and hiding the ends inside apply to soft sculpting as well.

Hidden Ladder Stitch

After stuffing, a fully jointed teddy bear has six openings which must be closed by hand. If correctly done, the hidden ladder stitch will close these openings with invisible stitches.

Work from the rightside, through only one thickness. Do not turn the seam allowances under before stitching. As the thread is pulled tight, the raw edges automatically turn to the inside.

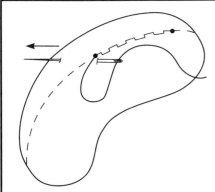

Fig. 3.12 After your final knot, insert your needle into the bear, bringing it out several inches away. Pull tightly and snip the thread right at the fabric backing.

Begin by securely knotting the thread and poking the needle from the wrongside to the rightside on the seam line (Fig. 3.13, point #1). Insert the needle in the opposite side, directly in line with the starting point, and take a stitch 3/16" or less (Fig. 3.13, points #2 and 3). If you are right-handed, work all stitches from right to left. The needle stays parallel to the raw edges.

Continue to alternate stitches from one side to the other. Fig. 3.13 diagrams the placement of the stitches. Actually, the stitches disappear when the thread is tightened (Fig. 3.14).

On a large opening, such as the body, you may lock your stitch every three or four inches. This holds the tension without a knot. A lock stitch is

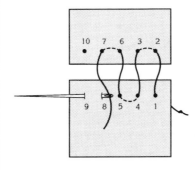

Fig. 3.13 Close the stuffing openings by hand with a hidden ladder stitch.

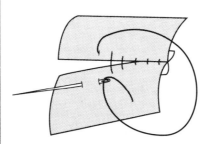

Fig. 3.14 The stitches of a properly sewn hidden ladder stitch disappear when the thread is tightened.

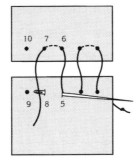

Fig. 3.15 For large openings, tighten thread after a few inches. Then lock your stitches by working one stitch from left to right.

the one time you work from left to right. Pull the thread tightly before starting the lock stitch. Fig. 3.15 shows the first half of the lock stitch being made from point 8 back to point 5. The next stitch is made once again at points 6

and 7. Continue with the hidden ladder stitch at points 8 and 9 as in the original Fig. 3.13.

After closing the entire opening, tighten and knot the thread at the last stitch. Lose the thread ends inside the bear by inserting the needle next to the knot and poking through the stuffing. Come out a couple of inches away, pull on the thread, and then clip (Fig. 3.12).

Features and Expressions

What will you like most about bearmaking? Creating the bear's face. I've never met a bearmaker who didn't adore making their teddy bears' faces. Let's discuss how to create memorable teddy bear personalities. It all starts with the features.

Safety Eyes

I feel strongly about this controversy, so I'm tackling it head on: A teddy bear is, first and foremost, a child's toy. Granted, adults own most of my bears, but I do whatever I can to assure my bears are as child-safe as I can make them.

A number of teddy bear artists disagree with me, and make bears exclusively for adult collectors. They use glass eyes for their creations, citing the facts that glass eyes are authentic and that plastic eyes scratch. I feel the child-safety aspects far outweigh the scratching considerations.

A friend of mine, while examining another artist's glass-eyed bear, grasped an eye and lifted it to see how tightly it was attached. To her mortification, the eye shattered, and she apologized profusely. The maker, also embarrassed, said the eye must have been defective. But imbedded in the fur was the eye's wire shank, covered with tiny shards of glass—a serious safety hazard.

Accidents happen. But when a child is injured by something loved and respected, like a teddy bear, and when that injury could have been avoided by using a different type of eye...well, enough said.

You don't need to sacrifice aesthetics for safety, either. The newer types of safety eyes look fantastic. Because glass eyes are hand-made, each is slightly irregular. In fact, many bearmakers purchase twenty or more glass eyes, and then match them up into appropriate pairs. Just because two eyes are on the same wire (Fig. 3.16) does not guarantee they're a matched set. On the other hand, the manufactured safety eyes are consistent.

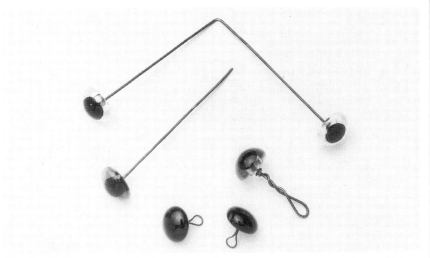

Fig. 3.16 Two types of glass eyes. One type comes on a wire, which is cut in the middle and twisted into a loop. The other has a preformed shank. Both are attached to the bear's head with heavy thread that's often anchored near the base of the ears. (Note: I never use glass eyes. See text.)

Fig. 3.17 My favorite safety eyes are a dark brown, translucent plastic. They look black in the package until you hold them to the light. They have a darker ring outlining the underside of the iris. These eyes come with metal lock washers.

I have not experienced many problems related to plastic eyes scratching. As you'll see in later chapters, invisible stitches sink the eyes on my designs, and the surrounding fiberfill and fur protect them. Of course, that won't help if the eye was scratched before or during installation.

Inside their packages, plastic eyes rub against each other and against the lock washers. To prevent further scratches, I store the eyes in a padded box, and keep the washers in a separate bag.

Safety eyes and noses come with either plastic or metal lock washers. Look for metal washers because they are easier to install, and they provide a stronger grip on the eye's shank. Some manufacturers have switched to plastic washers to prevent corrosion when the finished stuffed animal is washed. Although synthetic furs tolerate surface washing, you should never immerse your handmade bear in a tub of water.

The materials list for each bear will tell you what size eye to purchase (the diameter in millimeters). It will also specify either "black" or "animal" eyes. A black eye is solid, shiny black. An animal eye has a round, black pupil surrounded by a colored iris. Although animal eyes are available in more than twelve colors, I use the dark brown, translucent ones exclusively. See Fig. 3.17. Viewed against fur, these eyes sparkle and develop depth. They bestow lively, perky expressions on the bears. The Appendix lists a mail order source for these dark brown, standard plastic crystal eyes: Carver's Eye Co. Another brand is Zim's.

Regardless of the eye's size and color, its placement affects expression. This book's patterns mark the eye and nose locations because many readers will want to produce a bear like the photographs. Chapter 9 explains experimenting with different placements.

Covering the Nose

A fabric-covered nose looks much warmer and friendlier than a hard plastic one. I use a "D"-type triangular nose with a metal lock washer (Fig. 3.20), available from the same suppliers as the eyes. For the covering, the bear's directions will specify either coat wool or knit suede.

Coat wool has the same appearance as felt, but will wear much longer. Choose a heavy, black coating material (100% wool, Merino wool, or wool/mohair blend). The supply of quality coat woolens is seasonal, and they're expensive, but you need very little. Depending on the weave, the rightside may or may not have a nap. If in doubt, run your palm along the wool to see if both directions feel smooth. Align the arrow on the Nose pattern with the lengthwise grain of the fabric; it should point in the direction the fibers lay down. Coat wool stretches on the bias.

Not surprisingly, synthetic knit suede cloth (also called "Doe" suede) looks like brushed suede. This material works so well, you might think it was made specifically for covering

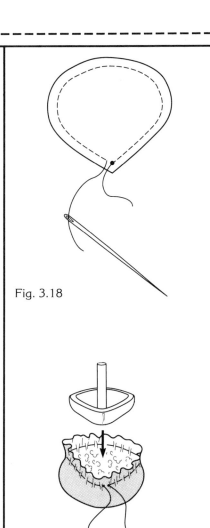

Fig. 3.18

Fig. 3.19

teddy bear noses. It does not ravel, is supple and easy to work with, and is economically priced. Most of the patterns use black because the color choice is limited. (For a light cream or white bear, substitute a finely woven, dark brown wool instead of black knit suede.) Pay attention to the stretch of the material rather than the nap. The fabric should be stable in the direction of the lengthwise grainline; the stretch runs across the piece.

The basic techniques for covering noses apply to all fabrics, regardless of size.

1. Find the rightside of your black coat wool or knit suede and determine whether it has a nap. Cut one Nose pattern (each bear has his own) from the fabric, matching the grainline arrow.

2. Thread your 3-1/2" needle with a doubled length of heavy-duty thread; knot 6" from the ends. Make a gathering line of small running stitches 1/8" from the raw edges of knit suede. (Sew slightly more than 1/8" in from the coat wool edges). (Fig. 3.18)

3. Partially tighten the gathers, keeping the material rightside

Fig. 3.20 Shown in two sizes with metal lock washers, these triangular, "D"-type noses will be covered with material before installation.

Fig. 3.21

out. Stuff the fabric with a small amount of fiberfill, and insert a "D"-type plastic nose on top of the fiberfill. (Fig. 3.19)

4. Draw the gathers tight. The shank will extend out the back of the covered nose. (Fig. 3.21)

5. Knot the thread securely and make several crossing stitches from opposite sides (much like an asterisk) to further close the gathers. Tie off. (Fig. 3.22)

6. To prevent raveling, coat the raw edges on the back of the nose with white glue. (Fig. 3.23)

Installing Eyes and Noses

To prevent scratching the eyes, pad your work surface with sheet rubber (Fig. 2.1) or folded fabric. Both the eyes and the nose are installed in the same manner:

1. With an awl, poke a hole in the face where marked. Poke from the wrongside, all the way through. Point the awl away from your body for safety. Ideally, the awl should separate the material's threads without breaking them, but don't fret if you hear a thread snap. (Fig. 3.24)

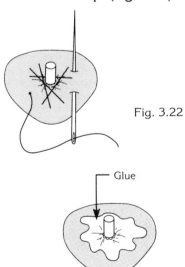

Fig. 3.22

Glue

Fig. 3.23

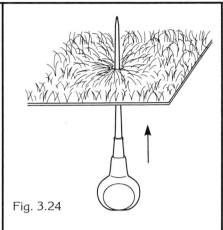

Fig. 3.24

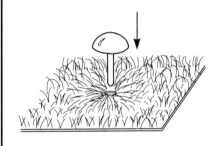

Fig. 3.25

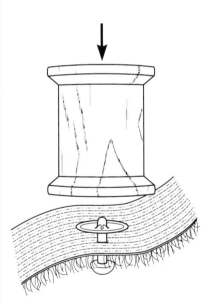

Fig. 3.26 Install the lock washer with its teeth pointing up, toward the tip of the shaft. Tighten the washer with the help of a wooden spool.

2. With the shaft of the awl in the material, smooth the fibers away from the hole on the rightside. The pile should radiate out from the hole.

3. Remove the awl and push the shaft of the eye or covered nose through the hole. Try not to trap any pile under the nose or the eyes. (Fig. 3.25)

4. Put the nose or eye rightside down on your rubber piece. Make sure you have the nose triangle properly oriented. (The eyes don't have a top and bottom, so you don't need to worry about them shifting.)

5. Place the washer on the shaft with its teeth up. Push the washer partially down the shaft. Slip a wooden spool onto the shaft and, with the palm of your hand, force the washer down as tightly as possible. (Fig. 3.26) The object is to get that washer on without bending it out of shape. Once installed, it should be hard to force your thumbnail under the eye and nose edges on the rightside.

Your first few eyes and noses might be tricky because they may rock while you shove the washer on them. Once you get the hang of it, you shouldn't have any further trouble, and I think it's grand fun—one of my favorite steps.

Squeakers

A voice adds a lively dimension to a stuffed bear. Before automatically inserting a squeaker into a hand puppet, though, consider the comment by one of my students, a former kindergarten teacher. She said if you hand a child a puppet with a squeaker, and then talk to the puppet, the puppet only answers back with a "squeak, squeak." Without a squeaker, the child furnishes the puppet's voice himself, which contributes to language development, play value, and interaction.

I have, however, provided directions for an optional, flat squeaker in the easy hand puppet, Fidget (Chapter 4). See Fig. 3.27. Although excluded from the directions, squeakers may also be inserted into Bearly Adequate's or Wispy's paws. Pad the squeakers with fiberfill so that you cannot feel their outline against the fur.

Now that you have the basics, are you ready to start? Pick one of the beginning patterns and become a bearmaker.

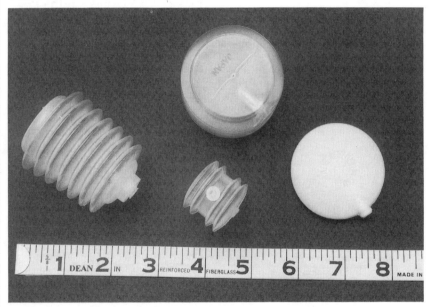

Fig. 3.27 Squeakers come in different shapes. The flat types have either a single or a dual noise.

4. Fidget

Hand Puppet With Squeaker and Stocking

**Finished height: 10"
(See color pages.)**

Fidget has a secret: the lining of this hand puppet is actually a pocket—just the right size for tucking away a six-year-old's private notes, trinkets, or other treasures.

That special pocket hides its own secret—a squeaker. Move Fidget with your thumb, first, and second fingers, as with an ordinary puppet. Your ring and baby fingers reach right inside the pocket, and, like magic, press the squeaker against the palm of your hand. Presto! Fidget has a voice all his own.

Before starting this puppet, read the previous two chapters and the following directions for an overall view.

Fur Selection Guide:

Choose a knit fur with a soft, pliable backing because your hand will be inside, against the wrongside of the fabric. (Furs are discussed further in Chapter 2.) The models were stitched in variegated furs with smooth, even piles measuring 7/16".

Upholstery velvet makes ideal paw pads, but Ultrasuede® or no-wale corduroy also work. In natural light, view several pad materials with your fur. Note how the paw pad color coordinates with and complements the fur. Base your choice on color first, fabric type second. You may reinforce lightweight fabrics, such as Facile® or robe velour, by fusing them to a lightweight interfacing.

Materials:

1/4 yd knit-backed fur (60" wide), pile height 3/8" to 1/2"

Small piece of coordinating material for paw pads

One pair 12mm brown animal eyes with lock washers

One 21mm "D"-type animal nose with lock washer

Small piece of black knit suede to cover nose

1/4 yd medium-weight cotton fabric for lining

One flat plastic squeaker, about 2" in diameter (optional: see note, page 22)

Polyester fiberfill

One plastic, "magnetic" hair roller, 1" diameter

One rubber band

1/3 yd grosgrain ribbon, 7/8" wide

Pattern Pieces:

Make a full set of pattern templates from the patterns on pages 40 to 43. You should have a total of ten pieces. (Directions for making master patterns start on page 9.)

Cutting Directions: *Follow the fur layout diagram.*

See page 11 for layout pointers.

Fur Fabric: Using the cutting techniques given on page 12, cut one Face, one Head Back, four Ears, two Body Backs (one reversed), and one Body Front.

Paw Pads: Cut two Paw Pads from appropriate material.

Lining: Make a long, crosswise fold down the center of the 1/4 yd cotton material. Cut one Lining Front, one Lining Back, and one Roller Cover, placing all on the fold where indicated. Position the Roller Cover against the selvage.

Transfer all pattern markings. Check page 11 if you need help on this step.

First Pinning: *Pin rightsides together, with raw edges even, tucking all pile to the inside. Insert pins at a right angle to the seam line.*

1. Pin the muzzle section of the Face to the main Face piece, matching the dots on both sides of the cutting line (these dots are close to the eyes). You will need to ease the muzzle section to fit between the eye and the center front seam on each side. (Fig. 4.2)

2. Pin the Body Backs together along the center back seam below the dot. (Fig. 4.3)

3. Pin two Ear pieces together along the curved edges. Repeat for the other Ear. (Fig. 4.4)

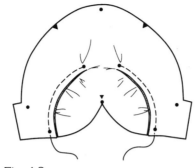

Fig. 4.2

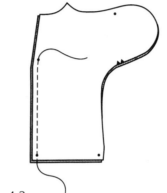

Fig. 4.3

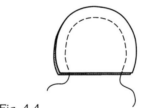

Fig. 4.4

Fig. 4.5

First Stitching: *All seam allowances are 1/4".*

1. Seam the muzzle section of the Face from the dots to the center front edges on both sides. (Fig. 4.2)

2. Stitch the Body Backs along the center back seam line, leaving open above the dot. (Fig. 4.3)

3. Seam an Ear along the curved upper edge, leaving the bottom edges open for turning. Likewise, seam the second Ear. Turn both rightsides out. (Fig. 4.4)

4. Make two darts in Body Front: fold on the solid lines, stitch on the broken lines. Try not to trap any pile on the rightside along your stitching line. (Fig. 4.5)

Second Pinning:

1. Pin the Face center front seam. (This seam is actually a dart that runs from just below the nose to the neck edge.) Carefully match the muzzle seams as you pin. (Fig. 4.6)

2. Pin a Paw Pad to the Body Front along the straight, un-notched arm edge. Repeat for the other Paw Pad. (Fig. 4.7)

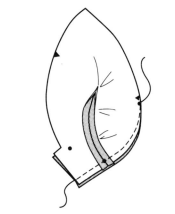

Fig. 4.6

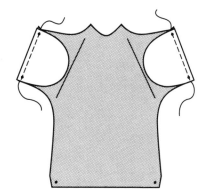

Fig. 4.7

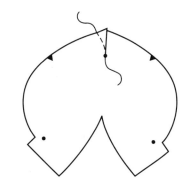

Fig. 4.8

Second Stitching:

1. Seam the Face center front seam from the dot below the nose to the neck edge. (Fig. 4.6)

2. Seam the Paw Pads to the Body Front from dot to dot. (Fig. 4.7)

3. Make the dart at the top of the Head Back. (Fig. 4.8)

Eyes and Nose:

Cover the nose with the knit suede material according to the directions on page 20.

Following the instructions on page 21, install the eyes and nose at the appropriate marks on the Face. Avoid trapping pile under the eyes or nose.

Third Pinning:

1. Pin the Face to the Head Back, matching the dot at the top of the Face to the dart on the Head Back. Match the notches and ease the Face to fit along the cheeks. Do not pin the neck edges. (Fig. 4.9)

2. Pin the Body Front to the Body Back along the shoulder, arm, paw pad, and side seams, matching double notches and dots. Don't pin the neck or bottom edges. (Fig. 4.10)

3. Pin the cotton Lining Front to the Lining Back at the two side seams. (Fig. 4.11)

4. Fold the Roller Cover along the "place on fold" line. Pin along the top and side seam. (Fig. 4.12)

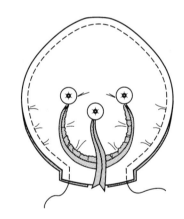

Fig. 4.9

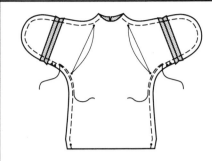

Fig. 4.10

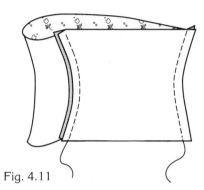

Fig. 4.11

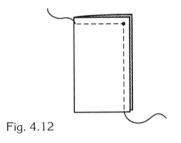

Fig. 4.12

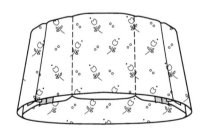

Fig. 4.13

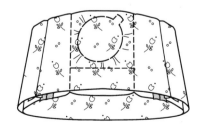

Fig. 4.14

Third Stitching:

1. Seam the Face to the Head Back, leaving the neck open. (Fig. 4.9)

2. Seam the body along the entire side seams. Leave open along the neck and bottom edges. To reinforce the curve at the underarms, stitch again over first stitching. Clip curves at underarms. (Fig. 4.10)

3. Stitch the Lining Front to the Lining Back along the side seams. (Fig. 4.11)

4. Stitch the Roller Cover across the top and side seams, pivoting stitching at the dot. Leave open at the bottom edge (selvage). (Fig. 4.12)

Lining and Squeaker:

Press the lining's side seam allowances open. Fold the lining in half on the "Place on fold" lines, wrongsides together. Press the fold line.

Sew the stitching lines as marked on the Front Lining (Fig. 4.13). Insert the flat plastic squeaker between the two layers of Front Lining, pushing the squeaker up to the inside fold line. Using a zipper foot, stitch across the lining from one stitching line to the other. The stitching should trap the squeaker in the top center front (Fig. 4.14).

Machine baste the raw edges of the lining together. With rightsides together, pin the lining to the body, matching center back and side seams. Stitch in a 1/4" seam (Fig. 4.15). Turn the lining to the inside, folding the body along the hem line. Note that this line is above, rather than on, the stitching line. Tack the lining to the body at the center back and underarm seam allowances. Leave the front lining free for a secret pocket between the lining and body.

Attaching the Head:

Turn the head rightside out. With the body still inside out, insert the head into the body. The rightsides of the fur should be together. Pin, matching the neck edges, easing the body to fit.

Stitch the neck seam, leaving the head and body open along the center back edges. (Fig. 4.16)

Turn the body and arms to the rightside. Check all the seams for trapped pile. (See page 14.)

Stuffing:

Stuff the front half of the head firmly. With your screwdriver or stuffing stick, pack extra fiberfill into the muzzle area to extend the nose for a good profile. Pressing fiberfill into the muzzle will take a considerable amount of force, so do it aggressively.

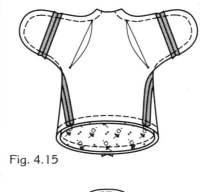

Fig. 4.15

Fig. 4.16

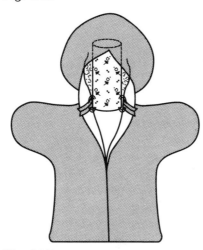

Fig. 4.17

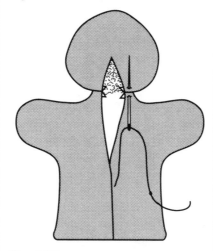

Fig. 4.18

Insert the hair roller into the Roller Cover. Hold the fabric temporarily in place with a rubber band. Position the covered roller inside the head with the enclosed end at the top. The bottom (open end) of the roller should be close to the neck edges.

Using upholstery thread, securely tack the roller and Roller Cover in place, sewing through a hole in the roller. Loop the thread around the edge of the roller several times, attaching it to the neck seam allowances at one side seam; knot. Repeat at the opposite side of the neck edge (Fig. 4.17). Snip and remove the rubber band.

Stuff the rest of the head, packing fiberfill on either side of the roller to fill out the cheeks nicely. Finish stuffing by adding fiberfill at the top of the roller, and stuff the back of the head until it is rounded when viewed from the side.

Closing the Back Opening:

Use the 3-1/2" needle and a doubled length of carpet or upholstery thread for this hand stitching.

1. Form a secure knot in your thread, leaving a 6" tail on the knot. To reinforce the closure at the center back neck edge, insert your needle from the rightside, 1/4" in from the raw edges, just below the neck seam. Take a 1/4" vertical stitch (going through the neck seam allowances). (Fig. 4.18)

2. From the rightside, insert your needle in the opposite side of the back opening, just above the neck seam. Take a 1/4" stitch on that side, also going through the neck seam allowances. (Fig. 4.19)

3. Draw these two stitches together, closing the opening around the end of the hair roller. Poke the back seam allowances to the inside; tighten. Knot your thread to the 6" tail extending from your beginning stitch. Cut the threads about 2"

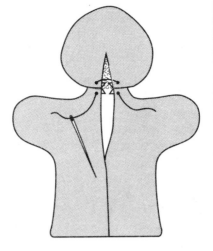

Fig. 4.19

from the puppet and tuck the threads inside the head.

4. Knot your thread again, this time at its end, and bring it up at the top of the center back opening. Working from the rightside of your material, close the head opening using a hidden ladder stitch (page 18). Knot your thread again at the neck, and continue to close the center back body opening. Knot the thread at the center back seam allowance (inside the puppet).

Sculpting the Face:

1. Mark the mouth with a quilting pin at each side. Using a tape measure, find the location for the first pin by measuring 7/8" down from the bottom of the nose and 1/8" to the left of the center seam. Place the second pin 1/8" to the right of the seam. (The pins should be 1/4" apart, and correspond to points 3 & 4 in Fig. 4.20.)

2. Thread the 5" needle with a long, doubled length of heavy-duty thread. When you take a stitch on the rightside of the fur, use the tip of the needle to pull out any pile that might be trapped. The pile should hide all your stitches.

3. Form a secure knot 6" from the ends of your thread. Insert your needle at the base of the muzzle, just below the chin dot (point 1). Bring the needle out at the inside corner of the eye (point 2). (Fig. 4.21)

4. Insert the needle close to the eye, taking a stitch about 1/8" long. Bring the needle out at point 3. (Fig. 4.22) To begin shaping, push down on the eye with your thumb as you pull on the thread.

5. Take a 1/4" stitch, inserting your needle at point 4. Remove the pins.

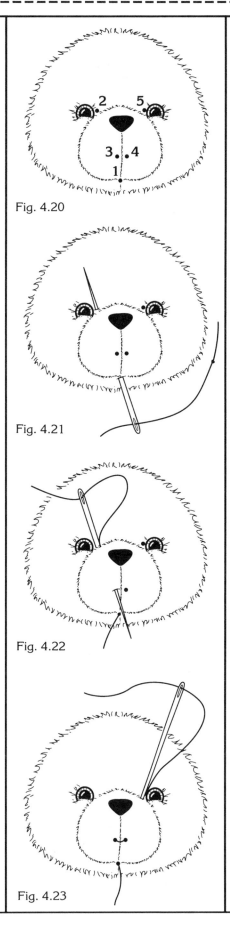

Fig. 4.20

Fig. 4.21

Fig. 4.22

Fig. 4.23

6. Bring the needle up at point 5 and take a stitch at the inside corner of this eye, as you did with the first eye (Fig. 4.23). Take a stitch inside the muzzle, coming out at point 4 again. Pull on your thread, pressing the eye down.

7. Continue to sculpt and shape the muzzle and the fiberfill as you work. From point 4, insert your needle at point 3. Come out at point 2. Take a stitch at point 2, bring the needle out at the chin (point 1). Take a short stitch, bringing the needle up at point 5. Take a stitch and go back to point 1. This time, after a short stitch, bring the needle through the fiberfill to the "bridge" of the muzzle, between the eyes. Make a 1/2" stitch in the fold of the fur to define the top of the muzzle, delineating it from the forehead. Bring your needle out next to your knot at point 1.

8. When happy with your bear's expression, knot your thread to the 6" tail. Lose the ends of your working thread inside the head (see page 18). Then thread the 6" tails on your shorter needle and hide them inside in the same manner.

Clipping the Muzzle:

1. Shorten the pile on the top of the muzzle (above the nose, between the eyes) by clipping it to half its height. Work conservatively, taking small snips at a time. You may want to practice on a scrap of fur first.

2. The shape of the eyes, not the mouth, determines this puppet's expression. It's easy to capture smiling eyes. First, if any pile covers the upper eye, trim it. For the lower part of the eye, shape the pile so that the eye looks like Fig. 4.24.

Attaching the Ears:

1. Close the bottom of the ears with the hidden ladder stitch (page 18). Turn the raw edges to the inside as you work. Pull on your thread to gather the bottom of the ear slightly before knotting it. Form a hollow in the ear by shaping it around the tip of your thumb.

2. The ear placement affects the bear's expression, so pin the ears in several different locations and decide where you want them. Compare your placement to the pictures in this book. Mark your preferred

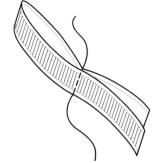

Fig. 4.24

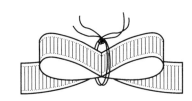

Fig. 4.25

Fig. 4.26

Fig. 4.27

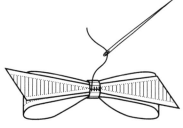

Fig. 4.28

Fig. 4.29

location temporarily with quilting pins.

3. Sew the ears securely to the head, curving the tops of the ears forward to form a crescent shape. Knot at both edges of the ears. Hide the ends of your threads inside the head, and remember to remove all the pins.

Bow Tie:

1. Fold a 10" length of grosgrain ribbon (7/8" wide) in half crosswise, wrongsides together.

2. Measure 2-3/4" from the fold; machine stitch across the ribbon (Fig. 4.25). Finger press the seam open on both sides.

3. Bring the fold down to meet the seam, forming two loops. Wrap the center with doubled upholstery thread. (Fig. 4.26) Tie thread ends with a surgeon's square knot (page 17). Trim the ribbon ends at a 45° angle. (Cut ends should be parallel.) (Fig. 4.27)

4. Fold a 1-5/8" length of ribbon in thirds, lengthwise, forming a strip just over 1/4" wide. Loop this strip around the center of the bow, covering the thread; overlap the ends in back. (Fig. 4.28) With upholstery thread, overcast the ends to secure; knot. Use the same thread to tack the bow tie to the center front of the puppet's body. (Fig. 4.29)

Christmas Stocking

**Finished size: 16"
(See color pages.)**

What better way to package a teddy bear gift than in his own Christmas stocking? This personalized stocking will make a charming gift, whether paired with your handmade bear or a ready-made puppet or bear.

This stocking, which uses odds and ends of ribbons and trims, is pieced in an ingenious way that looks as if the ribbons are interwoven with the fabric strips. The combinations are endless.

- Use Christmas print fabrics with solid red, white, and green ribbons.
- Try piecing strips without the ribbons.
- Instead of ribbon, stitch rows of lace on top your fabrics, parallel to the stitching lines of the strips (not perpendicular).

- Make a couple of your strips in Aida, and chart "Beary Merry Christmas" in a straight line. Repeat the words in a continuous line down the center of the strip. (Use the Christmas heart chart, page 85, as a guide for the lettering.)
- For a shortcut, purchase pre-quilted material rather than piecing your own. The pre-quilted material may be used for the entire stocking, or just for the stocking back.

Counted Cross Stitch

Skip these general directions if you're an experienced cross stitcher, and go directly to the Christmas Stocking's materials list.

If you have never done counted cross stitch, you will be pleased at how easy embroidery can be. The "secret" is the special, evenweave fabric that almost guarantees even stitches and a beautiful finished project. Watching your design take shape on an unmarked piece of fabric is fascinating.

The most popular evenweave fabrics are Aida and Hardanger. The thread count per inch of fabric determines the size of the finished design. Some beginners prefer to start with 11 or 14 count fabric. The same charts are used for all sizes.

Supplies for Cross Stitch:

Evenweave fabric

DMC 6-strand embroidery floss in colors listed on the charts

Tapestry needle (#26 for Hardanger, either #24 or #26 for Aida)

Masking tape (optional)

Embroidery hoop (optional)

Embroidery Directions:

1. Some charts have tables listing the design area's measurements. Add several inches of margin to these sizes before cutting the fabric. For example, adding 6" gives a 3" margin on each side. After cutting, bind the edges with masking tape, overcast them, or treat them with Fray Check™ to prevent raveling.

2. Separate a length of floss into three strands for 11 count fabric, two strands for 14 or 18 count, or one strand for 22 count.

3. The arrows mark the centers of the charts. Determine your starting point by counting out from the center of your fabric.

4. Take the first stitch from back to front, holding the tail of the thread behind the fabric. Work the first few stitches over this end to secure it.

5. Make one cross stitch for each square of the chart. For even stitches, pass the tapestry needle from back to front, then from front to back, "stabbing" rather than "sewing" in and out.

6. For a row of stitches the same color, first work diagonally from left to right. Complete the cross stitches from right to left (Fig. 4.31). All your stitches should be crossed in the same direction.

7. End off by running the thread under stitches on the back of the work.

8. Some charts' squares are split diagonally into two colors. Fig. 4.32 shows how to make these 1/4 or 3/4 stitches. A #26 tapestry needle pierces the fabric easiest.

9. After cross stitches are completed, backstitch the chart's heavy outlines (Fig. 4.33). Use two strands for the backstitch on 11 count fabric, and only one strand for the other sizes of fabric.

10. Even if the finished piece looks clean, always wash it to remove hidden oils from your hands. Soak the embroidery in cold water with a mild detergent. Rinse well, and blot between white or light, colorfast towels. When nearly dry, block with a warm iron by pressing gently, face down, on a well-padded surface. (See "Block" in Glossary.)

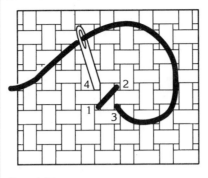

Fig. 4.30

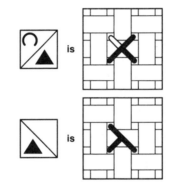

Fig. 4.31

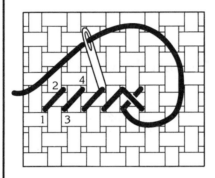

Fig. 4.32

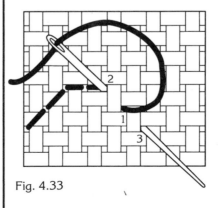

Fig. 4.33

Materials for Christmas Stocking:

1/8 to 1/4 yd each of five or more 100% cotton fabrics (see Strips for Quilting on the next page)

1/4 yd Aida (See cuff embroidery directions for which size Aida to use. Generally, names of less than six letters are worked on 11 count, names of seven to eight letters use 14 count, and up to 10 letters fit on 18 count Aida.)

Embroidery floss in three colors to coordinate with fabric strips. Mine was stitched in DMC 304 (scarlet), 701 (green), and 603 (pink), but select colors to match your fabrics.

1/8 yd cotton or other material for cuff lining (match the color of your Aida)

1/2 yd cotton fabric for stocking lining

1/2 yd light pink gingham, 1/4" check

1/2 yd fleece

1/2 yd each of approximately 15 different ribbons, 1/8" to 1" wide

1-1/4 yd piping

Graph paper

20" of 1/4" dowel (optional, to support the puppet's head)

Strips for Quilting:

Prewash 100% cotton fabrics. Cut or tear long, crosswise strips of fabric 1-1/2" wide. If strips are torn, iron the edges. The fabric requirements for the pictured model were:

1/8 yd each of scarlet and dark green

1/4 yd each of pink and light green

3/8 yd white (Note: The gingham showed through my stocking's white fabric, so the white strips were sewn double thickness. Also, 3/8 yd included enough extra to line the cuff.)

Pattern Pieces:

The main Stocking piece (page 44) may be enlarged by hand or with the help of a photocopy machine. To enlarge by hand, transfer each square of the graph onto a 12" by 18" (or larger) sheet of paper, ruled in 1" squares. To enlarge by photocopying, first make one copy the same size as the book's page. Divide the photocopy into quarters by cutting along the heavier lines on the grid. Enlarge each section individually by photocopying twice at 130% each time. To correct any copy machine distortion, align the final four 8-1/2" by 11" pages and measure your pattern. The top of the stocking should be 9" wide, and the vertical height from the base of the toe to the

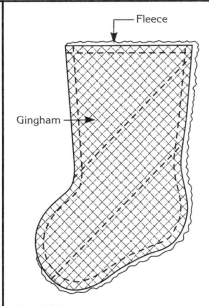

Fig. 4.34

top edge should be 17". Adjust where necessary and then tape the four sections together to form one pattern piece.

The Stocking Loop and the Stocking Cuff are shown full-size and may be either photocopied or traced directly from the book.

Cutting Directions:

Cut one Stocking Loop from one of the quilt strip materials.

Cut one Stocking Cuff from the cotton lining that matches your Aida, placing on fold.

Cut two Stockings from the lining material.

Cut two Stockings from pink gingham, adding an extra 1" all the way around. Cut one at a time for a perfect match with the grainline arrow. To mark the line for the first strip (at the

toe), make a pencil mark in the 1" extra border at both sides. Do not mark the entire line.

Cut two Stockings from fleece, adding 1" all the way around.

Preparation for Quilting:

Place a gingham Stocking on top of one of the fleece pieces (Fig. 4.34). Hand baste the raw edges together. Also run a couple of hand basting lines on the diagonal of the stocking, perpendicular to the sewing line for the first strip. Use the lines of the gingham as a guide.

Repeat for the second gingham and fleece pieces, which should be a mirror image of the first set.

Piecing the Stocking Back:

For machine quilting, use a walking foot, if available. It will feed the layers of material and batting at the same rate. Use a short stitch length, about 12 or 14 stitches to the inch.

Organize your quilt strips adjacent to each other and preview the effect. Once you have determined the placement, write it down.

If using a very light pastel or a white strip, check to see if the gingham will show through it. If necessary, use a doubled thickness of the light fabric. Treat both thicknesses as one strip.

1. Place your first strip rightside up on the toe of the gingham-batting stocking back, matching the edge of the strip to the marks at either side for the first strip placement. Align the entire edge of the strip parallel to the gingham check. You don't need to have the edge of the strip aligned exactly with the edge of a checked line on the gingham. Simply use the gingham as a guide to keep your stitching line straight.

2. Pin the second strip face down on top of the first strip, raw edges even with the placement line. Give yourself a little extra strip material at both sides because the stocking widens. (Fig. 4.35)

3. Stitch the strips in a straight, 1/4" seam. You stitch through four layers: batting, gingham, and two strips. Backstitching at the beginning or end is unnecessary because the edges will later be trimmed.

4. Open the top strip and finger press flat. Trim the strips even with the cut edges of the gingham and fleece.

5. Place the third strip on top of the second strip, rightsides together, raw edges even. Make sure your strips are still aligned with the checks in the gingham. Stitch and open strip as before.

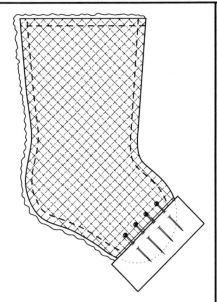

Fig. 4.35

6. Similarly, continue to add strips until you have reached the opposite top corner. The strips will completely cover the gingham.

Piecing the Stocking Front:

When working with the ribbons, you may want to place a few thin ribbons on top of wider ones. Treat these layered ribbon pairs as one ribbon. They don't need to be stitched together first. Since all ribbons are placed face down, position the narrow ribbon rightside down first, and center the wider ribbon face down on top of it.

The wrongside of the ribbon often resembles the rightside. An easy way to determine the rightside is to hold a few inches of the ribbon's free end horizontally. It should curl the way it was wound on the reel, which was rightside out.

Remember that the word "strip" refers to the cotton fabric, not the ribbons. Only the first strip is placed rightside up. All the other strips and ribbons are added rightside down. Use the gingham checks as a guide to keep the ribbons perpendicular to the stitching lines.

Place all pins at right angles to the stitching lines.

1. Place the first strip rightside up on the toe of the gingham-batting stocking front, one raw edge even with the marks for the first strip placement. Select ribbon #1 and place it perpendicular to the edge of the first strip, face down, in the middle of the strip. Pin it close to the start of the ribbon at the first strip placement line. The cut end of the ribbon should be even with the raw edge of the fabric strip.

2. Pin ribbon #2 perpendicular to, and face down on, the first strip. The distance between ribbon #1 and ribbon #2 should be 3/4" plus the width of ribbon #4 (which goes between them on the next strip). Pin ribbon #3, which should be 3/4" plus the width of ribbon #5 away from ribbon #1.

3. Place the second fabric strip face down on the first strip, sandwiching the ribbons in between. Again, remember to leave a little extra at the beginning of this strip because the stocking widens. Stitch in a 1/4" seam, keeping the ribbons perpendicular to the stitching line.

4. Open out the second strip and ribbons #1, 2, and 3. Finger press flat. Using the gingham as a guide to keep the ribbons perpendicular, temporarily pin the loose ends of these ribbons to the gingham. Trim the strips even with the cut edges of the gingham and fleece.

5. Pin ribbon #4 face down on the second strip, between ribbons #1 and 2. Pin ribbon #5 between ribbons #1 and 3.

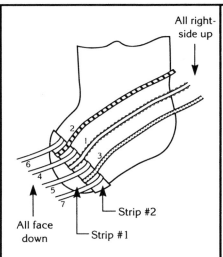

Fig. 4.36

Add ribbon #6 face down at one side, 3/8" away from ribbon #2. Ribbon #7 should be 3/8" away from ribbon #3 at the other side. (Fig. 4.36)

Don't despair—this first set of ribbons is the most confusing one. It gets much easier to keep track of the ribbons as you work up the stocking.

6. Place the third fabric strip face down on the second strip, raw edges even. Pin between the ribbons to hold this strip in position. Stitch. Cut ribbons #1, 2, and 3 even with the raw edges of the strips. Open out the third strip and ribbons #4,

5, 6, and 7. Finger press flat. Temporarily pin ribbons #4, 5, 6, and 7 to keep them perpendicular.

7. Pin ribbons #1, 2, and 3 face down on the third fabric strip, directly in line with where they began. They will overlap the same ribbons that are already sewn, but will appear to be woven in a straight line once they are turned rightside up. (If your ribbons are narrow, you may need to add ribbons #8 and 9 at either side of this strip.) Place the fourth strip face down on the third strip. Pin and stitch the fourth strip. Cut ribbons #4, 5, 6, and 7; then open out the fourth strip and its ribbons.

Continue to construct the stocking front, keeping your strips aligned with the gingham. Add new ribbons at each side as the stocking widens. You will probably need to add new ribbons about the sixth strip, and continue to add on one side of each row as you work towards the top. Discontinue adding ribbons at the top 3" that will later be covered by the cuff.

Final Pattern Cutting:

1. After completing the piecing, position the pattern piece on the front stocking. Adjust the location as desired, keeping the grainline arrow aligned with your strips. Pin the pattern and cut out the stocking front.

2. Lay the stocking front on top of the untrimmed stocking back, rightsides together. Line up the quilt strips, paying particular attention to the side seams and the top of the foot. The bottom of the foot and the stocking's top (that will later be covered by the cuff) are not as noticeable, so if your strips do not match, try to compensate in less noticeable areas. When you have matched the strips, pin the front to the back and cut out the back. Remove the pins.

3. Remove the diagonal hand basting threads from the gingham and backing on both the front and back stockings. Baste any loose ribbons or strips close to the cut edges.

Lining: *The seam allowances for the lining are 5/8".*

Pin the two stocking linings rightsides together. Stitch, leaving the top straight edges open. Trim seams; clip curves.

Piping:

Pin the piping to the rightside of the stocking front along the sides and bottom. The line of stitching on the piping should be 1/2" in from the raw edges. The cord of the piping goes toward the center; the piping seam allowances are on top of the stocking seam allowances.

Using a zipper foot, baste the piping to the stocking front, stitching right on top of the stitching line of the piping.

Stocking Seam: *The stocking seam allowances are 1/2".*

1. Pin the stocking front to the stocking back, rightsides together, sandwiching the piping in between. Match the quilt strips as closely as possible.

2. Stitch the seam with a zipper foot, following your previous basting line. Leave top edges open. To reduce bulk, grade seams; clip curves. Turn to rightside.

3. Check the piping. If the stitching line shows, or is uneven, turn the stocking inside out and restitch any problem areas. Turn to rightside again.

4. Insert the lining inside the stocking, wrongside of lining to wrongside of fleece. Align side seams. Baste the top edges of the stocking and lining together.

Loop:

1. Fold the stocking loop in half lengthwise, rightsides together. Pin along the long, notched edge. Stitch, leaving short sides open. Trim seam; turn rightside out. Bring the seam to the center and press.

2. Center a 5-1/8" length of 1/2"- to 3/4"-wide ribbon on the loop, covering the seam. Top stitch close to both edges of the ribbon.

3. Fold the loop in half, wrongsides together. Pin the loop at the center back top edge of the stocking, rightside of loop to rightside of lining, raw edges even. The loop will extend down inside the stocking. Baste raw edges together.

Counted Cross Stitched Cuff:

On graph paper, chart the person's name using the alphabet in this chapter. The lower case letters should connect to each other when there is a "tail" (for example, the letter "a" connects to the "b"). The letters are shown with approximately the correct spacing between them. The name "Laura" has been charted on the next page to give you an example. When in doubt on the placement, try to maintain a consistent spacing between the vertical rows of cross stitches that form the downstrokes of the letters, rather than worrying about the beginning and ending tails of each letter. Viewing your completed chart from a distance, evaluate how easily you can read the name, and decide whether you need to adjust the spacing.

After completing your own chart, count the number of stitches horizontally from the beginning letter of your charted name to the end of the last letter. If it is less than 60 spaces, use 11 count Aida. If it is 61 to 80 spaces, use 14 count Aida. If it is 81 to 100 spaces, use 18 count Aida.

Cut the Aida to measure 8" high by 21" wide. Overcast the edges, bind with masking tape, or treat with Fray Check™.

Find the center point of your graphed name and mark it on your chart. To position the name correctly, find the corresponding location on your Aida by measuring 6-3/4" in from the right edge and 4" down from the top. This is the center stitch of your name.

Following the counted cross stitch directions on pages 31-32, embroider the name with the predominant color.

Stitch the border under the name in the other two colors of floss. The bottom row of the border should be about 1-1/2" below the center point of your name. (The border is six spaces high. If your name has letters like lower case f, g, j, p, q, or y that extend downward, make sure that the top of your border will not crowd the letters. Adjust as necessary.) The finished border should measure 4-1/8" to the right of the center of the name, and 12-3/8" to the left.

Cuff:

1. Trim the finished Aida to size by aligning the center of the cross stitched name with the mark on the pattern piece. The bottom of the cross stitched border should be on the seam line, 1/2" above the cutting line. Use the pattern piece as a guide, but cut the Aida one layer at a time, following the weave of the material.

2. With rightsides together, pin the cuff lining to the Aida cuff along the long, notched bottom edge. Stitch in a 1/2" seam. Layer seam; press toward lining. Press top, unnotched edge of lining to the inside along seam line. Trim this pressed seam allowance to 1/4". Press the lining up, forming a crease in the Aida just below the counted cross stitched border. No unworked Aida should show below the stitches.

3. Open out the cuff lining again. Fold the cuff in half, rightsides together, matching the short sides of the Aida to itself and matching the lining to itself. Pin along the side seam leaving the top open; stitch. Press seam open. Grade seam allowances. Turn rightside out.

4. Place the cuff inside the stocking with the rightside of the Aida against the rightside of the lining. Align the midpoint of the cuff with one stocking seam, and match the cuff seam to the other stocking seam. Make sure the cross stitched name is at the front of the stocking, not the back. Pin the Aida layer of the cuff to the top edge of the stocking. (The cuff lining extends down inside the stocking for this step.)

5. Stitch the top edge of the stocking. To reinforce loop at center back, stitch again over first stitching. Grade seam. Pull cuff out and finger press seam toward cuff.

6. Fold the cuff lining to the inside along the cuff's bottom seam line. Pin the pressed edge of the cuff lining over the top stocking seam and slip stitch. Fold the finished cuff down and finger press along top seam.

Slip a teddy bear hand puppet in the top, and you have a delightful decoration for your mantel. To support the puppet's head, tuck a 20" length of 1/4" dowel inside (for display only—not play). Just one prediction: you'll find that teddy bear spending more time in someone's arms than in the stocking.

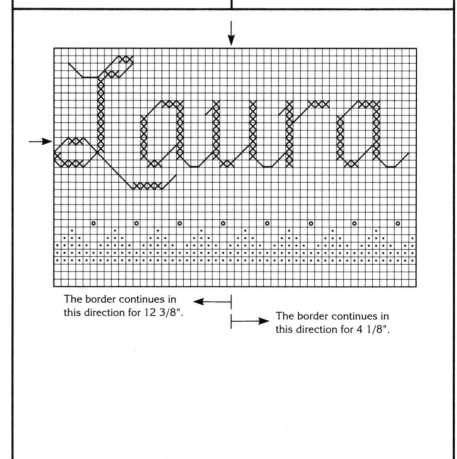

The border continues in this direction for 12 3/8".

The border continues in this direction for 4 1/8".

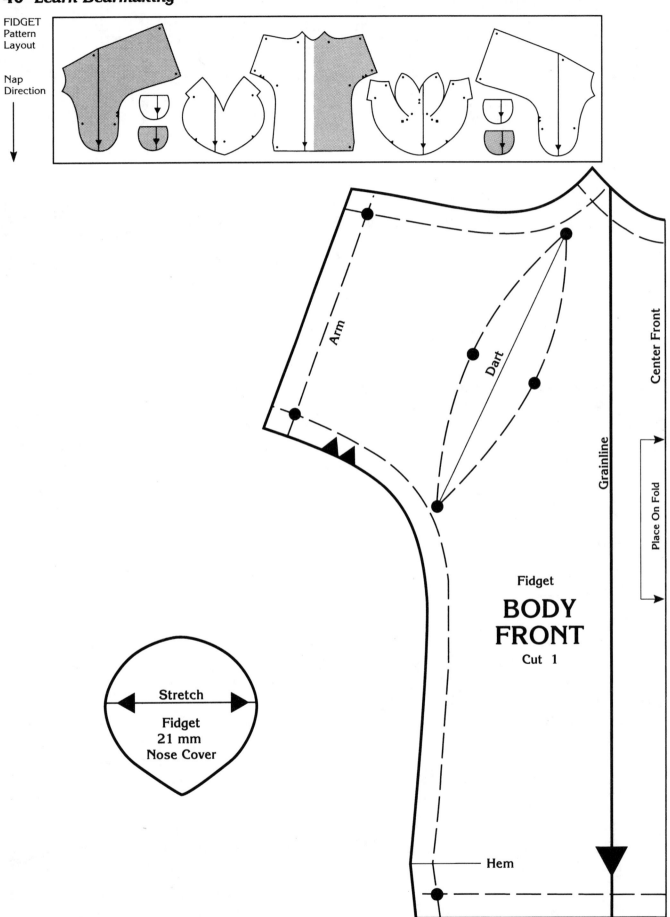

FIDGET
Pattern
Layout

Nap
Direction

Arm

Dart

Center Front

Grainline

Place On Fold

Fidget

**BODY
FRONT**

Cut 1

Hem

Stretch

Fidget
21 mm
Nose Cover

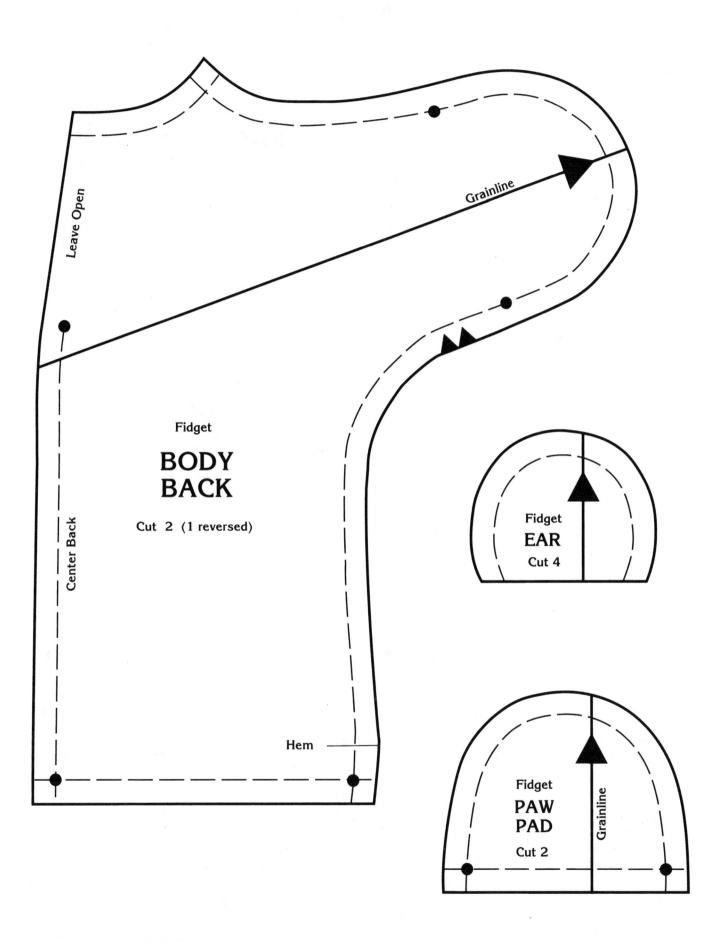

Leave Open

Grainline

Center Back

Fidget

BODY BACK

Cut 2 (1 reversed)

Hem

Fidget
EAR
Cut 4

Fidget
PAW PAD
Cut 2

Grainline

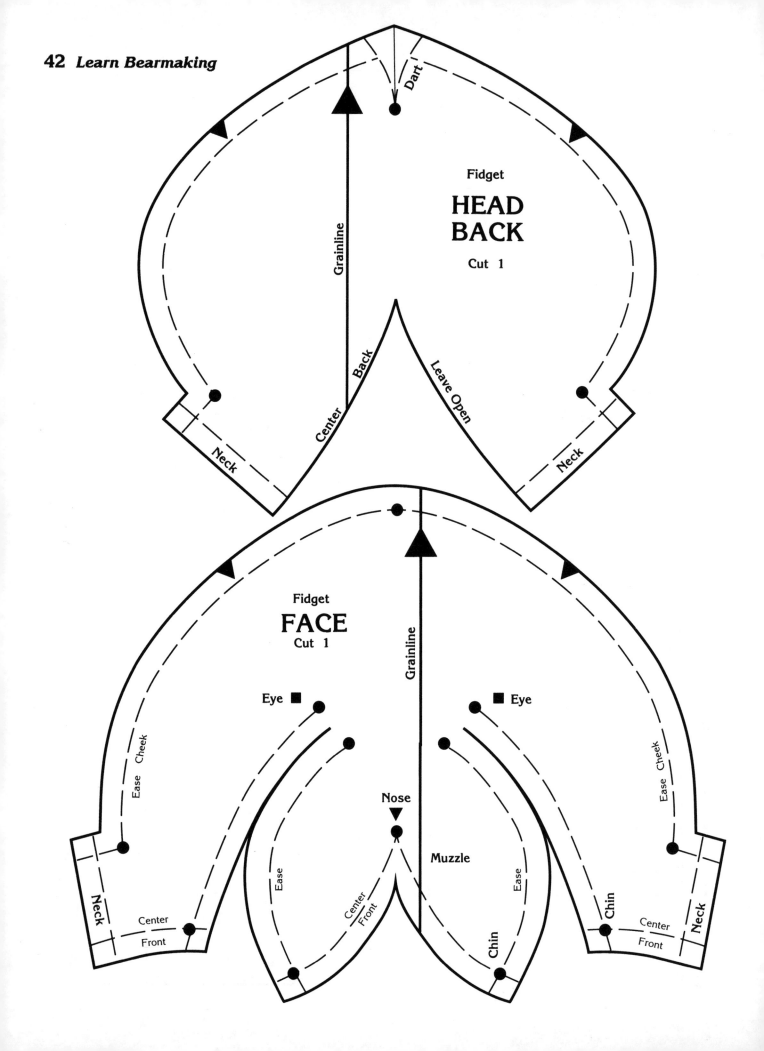

Dart

Fidget

HEAD
BACK

Cut 1

Grainline

Center Back

Leave Open

Neck

Neck

Fidget

FACE

Cut 1

Grainline

Eye ■

■ Eye

Ease Cheek

Ease Cheek

Nose ▼

Muzzle

Ease

Ease

Neck

Chin

Chin

Neck

Center

Center Front

Front

Center Front

Chin

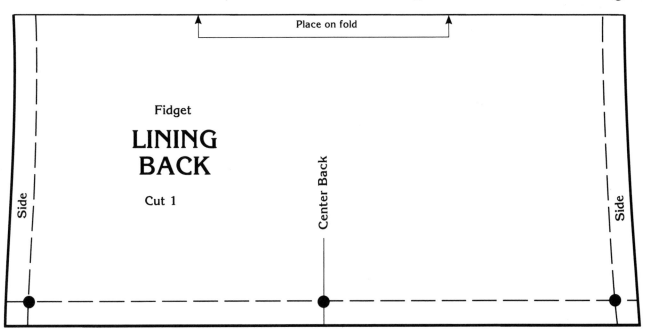

Fidget
LINING BACK
Cut 1

Place on fold

Side · Side · Center Back

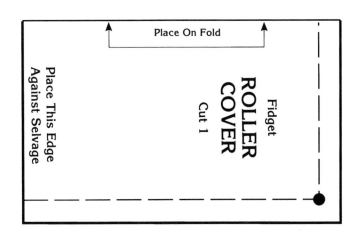

Fidget
ROLLER COVER
Cut 1

Place On Fold

Place This Edge Against Selvage

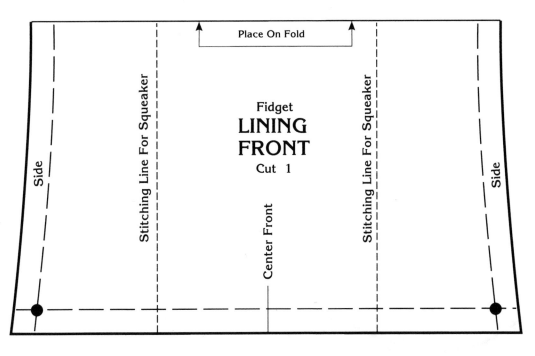

Fidget
LINING FRONT
Cut 1

Place On Fold

Side · Side · Center Front · Stitching Line For Squeaker · Stitching Line For Squeaker

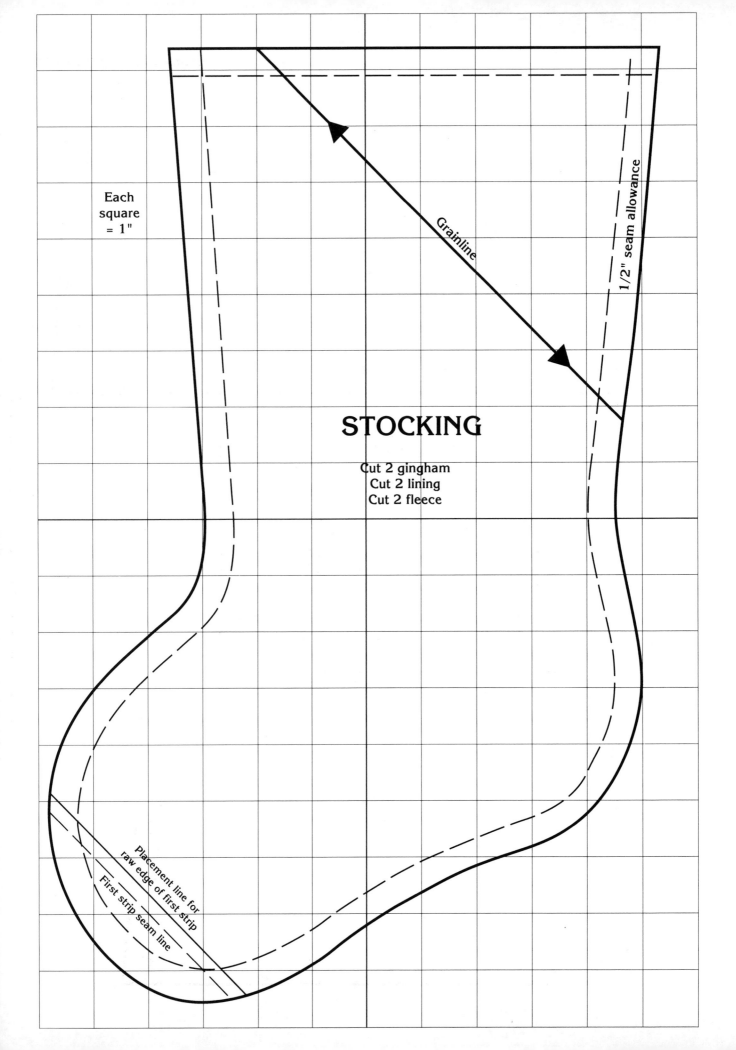

Each
square
= 1"

Grainline

1/2" seam allowance

STOCKING

Cut 2 gingham
Cut 2 lining
Cut 2 fleece

Placement line for
raw edge of first strip

First strip seam line

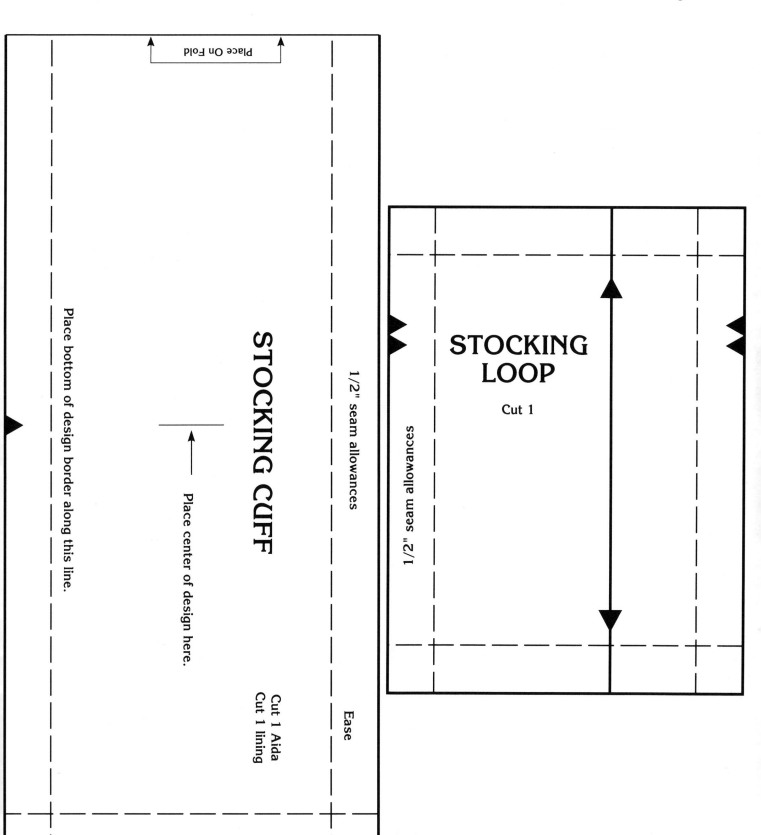

Place On Fold

1/2" seam allowances

STOCKING CUFF

Place center of design here.

Place bottom of design border along this line.

Ease

Cut 1 Aida
Cut 1 lining

STOCKING
LOOP

Cut 1

1/2" seam allowances

5. Wispy

Easy Non Jointed Bear

Finished height: 20"
(See color pages.)

Teddy bears are for hugging, and that's where Wispy excels. All teddy bears can be divided into two groups: jointed and nonjointed. Wispy is a non-jointed bear, which means the limbs and head do not rotate like the arms, legs, and heads

of the bears in the Intermediate and Advanced sections of this book. Instead, Wispy's arms and legs flop back and forth. A jointed bear has a distinct advantage for posing in different positions. But unjointed bears also have advantages. They're easier to make, and oh so cuddly.

For those who don't want to spend the time sewing clothes for their teddy bear, Wispy was designed to wear regular infant clothing, size 0-6 months. You may already have a baby outfit, or you can take Wispy shopping. For boys, choose shorts rather than long pants, and full-cut, short sleeves. A girl Wispy looks nice in a "diaper set"—a shorter-cut dress (elastic at sleeve edges) and matching, ruffled panties.

Wispy wears another item of infant apparel—disposable diapers. Size medium (for human babies 8-12 lbs.) fit nicely; just fold the diaper's top gathered edge to the inside.

Before starting Wispy, review the General Directions and Beginning Techniques, and read through the entire set of Wispy directions.

Fur Selection Guide:

You have three furs to coordinate for this bear: the main body fur, the fur for the muzzle and pads, and the ear wisps. The main fur must be huggable. More than any other pattern in this book, this cuddly bear needs a soft, silky, warmly inviting fur—a fur you have to touch. Fig. 2.9 illustrates two different main fur pile heights, 1-1/16" and 3/4". What you can't tell from a photo is that the shorter fur feels marvelously soft.

Once you have selected your main fur, coordinate a muzzle and paw pad fur. Since you need a pile height of only 3/8", check to make sure the fibers are dense and the backing does not show. If you have trouble finding an appropriate shorter-napped fur, you could use your main fur and shave the pile to a height of 3/8" by following the directions on page 64. This will, of course, give you a perfect color match. You will have plenty of main fur fabric from your 1/2 yd to use for the muzzle and pads without purchasing extra yardage.

When it comes to the ear wisp fur, select a 2" pile that contrasts with your main fur—either lighter or darker. You'll need to look at furs that are meant for "fabulous fake" fur coats. You may not recognize a suitable fur looking at a full bolt of it. Sometimes these materials are striped or variegated to simulate pieced pelts. Depending on where you position your pattern piece, the same bolt of subtly striped fur will offer several different color combinations. Remember, you need only a couple of inches for the small, triangular ear inserts. Check the list of suppliers at the end of the book if you have trouble locating this fur.

Materials:

Main Bear: 1/2 yd knit-backed fur fabric (60" wide), 3/4" to 1-1/16" pile height

Contrast Muzzle and Pads: 1/8 yd knit-backed fur fabric, 3/8" pile height

Ear Wisps (optional): small piece fur fabric with pile at least 2" long

One 24mm "D"-type plastic animal nose with lock washer

Small piece of black, heavyweight coating fabric, 100% wool or wool blend, to cover the nose

Two 15mm black eyes and lock washers

Polyester fiberfill

Pattern Pieces:

Make a full set of pattern templates from the patterns on pages 56-61. Notice that the Body Front and Body Back patterns are too large to fit on one page. You will need to piece together these two pieces for your master patterns, before you cut your fur. Follow the directions for making pattern templates on pages 9-10, paying particular attention to the section on piecing patterns together. You should have a total of 14 master pattern pieces.

Cutting Directions: *Follow the fur layout diagram.*

See page 11 for layout pointers.

Main Fur Fabric: Using the cutting techniques given on page 12, cut one Face, Body Front, and Seat. Cut two Body Backs, Head Backs, Arms, Tops of Feet, Front Ears, and Back Ears. Remember to reverse your pattern when you cut two of the same piece.

Note: For a bear without ear wisps, cut a total of four Ear Backs. Substitute your two extra Ear Backs for the Ear Fronts in the directions. Disregard references to Ear Inserts.

Notice that the Body Front has a center dart. The cutting line for this dart is curved away from the fold line at the end of the center front line. (This cutting line is about 1" long, and is thicker than the fold line.)

Shorter, Contrasting Fur: Cut two Foot Pads, two Paw Pads, and one Muzzle.

Long-napped Fur: Cut two Ear Inserts.

You should have 22 fur pieces for bears with ear wisps (15 in the main color, five in the contrasting, and two long-napped). Bears without ear wisps have 20 pieces.

Transfer all pattern markings. Check page 11 if you need help on this step.

Ear Wisps:

For the Ear Inserts with the long pile, trim the pile down to the backing for the outer 1/8" of the seam allowances. (You only want to reduce the amount of wispies. Do not trim the fabric backing itself or make the piece smaller.)

First Pinning: *Pin rightsides together, with raw edges even, tucking all pile to the inside. Insert pins at a right angle to the seam line.*

1. Pin one Ear Insert to an Ear Front, matching dots. Repeat for the other Ear Front. (Fig. 5.2)

2. Pin the appropriate Paw Pad to one Arm, matching double notches at wrists. Repeat for the other Arm. (Fig. 5.3)

3. Along the curved, unnotched edge, pin one Top of Foot to the Body Front at an ankle, matching dots. Repeat for other Top of Foot. (Fig. 5.4)

4. Pin two Head Back pieces together along unnotched, center back seam, above dot. (Fig. 5.5)

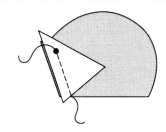

Fig. 5.2

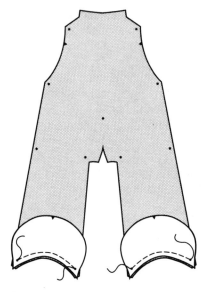

Fig. 5.4

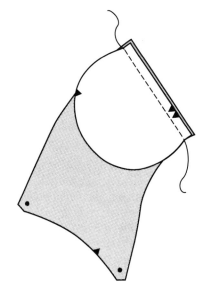

Fig. 5.3

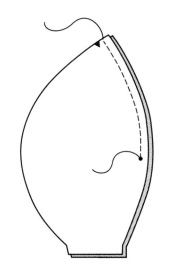

Fig. 5.5

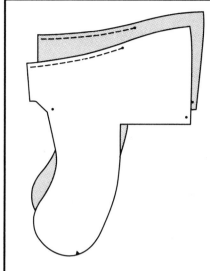

Fig. 5.6

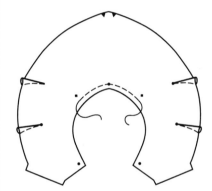

Fig. 5.7

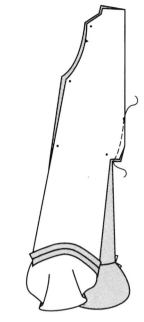

Fig. 5.8

First Stitching: *All seams allowances are 1/4".*

1. Seam Ear Inserts to Ear Fronts. (Fig. 5.2)

2. Seam Paw Pads to Arms along the straight seam lines at the wrists. (Fig. 5.3)

3. Seam Tops of Feet to Body Front along ankle lines. (Fig. 5.4)

4. Sew Head Backs together along center back seam, leaving open below dot. (Fig. 5.5)

5. Stay stitch each Body Back along the center back line, from the dot to the neck edge. (Fig. 5.6) (Stay stitching is a line of straight machine stitching, done on a single layer of fabric at a time, to prevent stretching. In this case, it should be slightly less than 1/4" from the raw edge.)

6. Stay stitch Face between eyes, along muzzle seam. Make four darts in Face. (To make darts, fold along solid lines, and stitch along broken lines from the wide part to the point.) (Fig. 5.7)

7. Make one dart in Body Front. (Fig. 5.8)

Second Pinning:

1. Pin an Ear Front (with the attached insert) to the corresponding Ear Back. Repeat for other ear. (Fig. 5.9)

2. Pin the tops of the Arms to the appropriate sides of the Body Front, matching notches and dots. (Fig. 5.10)

3. Pin Body Backs along center back, below dot. (Fig. 5.11)

4. Pin Muzzle to Face, matching three dots, easing the Muzzle to fit below the eyes on each side. (Fig. 5.12)

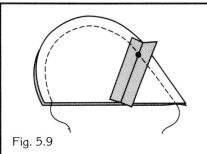

Fig. 5.9

Fig. 5.10

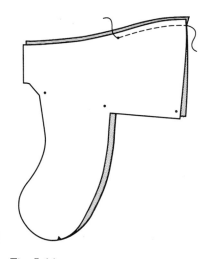

Fig. 5.11

Second Stitching:

1. Seam one Ear together along the curved top edges. Leave the bottom edges open. Repeat for the other ear. (Fig. 5.9)

2. Seam the top of an Arm to the Body Front from dot to dot. Repeat. (Fig. 5.10)

3. Sew the center back seam of the Body Backs, below dot. (Fig. 5.11)

4. Seam the Muzzle to the Face, from one chin dot to the other. (Fig. 5.12)

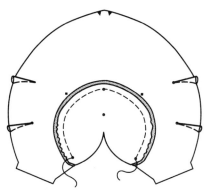

Fig. 5.12

Third Pinning:

1. Pin Body Backs to curved edge of Seat, matching centers and dots. (Fig. 5.13)

2. Pin the center seam of the Face, from the nose dot, through the chin dots, to the neck edge. (Fig. 5.14)

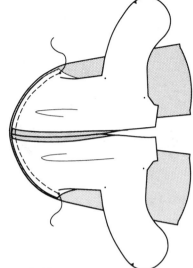

Fig. 5.13

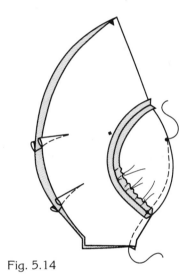

Fig. 5.14

Third Stitching:

1. Seam Body Backs to Seat from dot to dot. (Fig. 5.13)

2. Stitch the center Face seam from nose to neck. Taper the stitching at the nose like a dart. Do not seam neck edges. (Fig. 5.14)

Eyes and Nose:

Use the coat wool to cover the nose according to the directions on page 20.

Following the instructions on page 21, install the eyes and nose at the appropriate marks on the Face. Use care not to trap any pile under the eyes or nose.

Fourth Pinning:

1. Pin Face to Head Backs, matching notches and neck edges. Ease the Face to fit below the darts. (Fig. 5.15)

2. Pin the Body Front to the Body Back around the entire body and limbs. Match all notches and dots. Do not pin the neck edges or the feet. (If your material is too bulky, you may want to pin only half, sew it, and then pin the other half.) (Fig. 5.16)

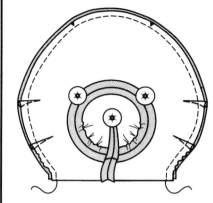

Fig. 5.15

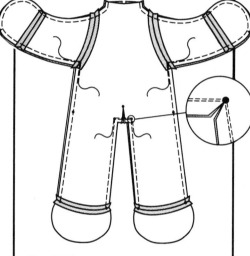

Fig. 5.16

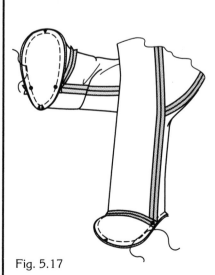

Fig. 5.17

Fourth Stitching:

1. Sew the side seams of the head, from one neck edge around to the other. Leave neck open. (Fig. 5.15)

2. Sew the front and back bodies together along the arms and side seams, and the inner leg seams. Where stitching pivots at the corners (dots at the top of the inner leg seams and under the arms), stitch again over the first stitching. Clip the seam allowances to these dots at the crotch and underarms. (Fig. 5.16)

Inserting the Foot Pads:

1. With sole side up and rightsides together, pin a Foot Pad to the bottom of each leg. Match all dots and notches. (Fig. 5.17)

2. Seam with leg side up. If your machine balks at sewing over the seam allowances at the side dots, finish those areas by hand.

Joining the Head to the Body:

1. Turn the head rightside out.

2. With the body still inside out, and with the head upside down, insert the head inside the body. Pin the head to the body along the neck edges, matching center fronts and back opening edges. (If you want your bear to turn his head to the side, offset the center front lines 3/8".) Ease the back to fit.

3. With head side up, stitch the neck edge. (Fig. 5.18)

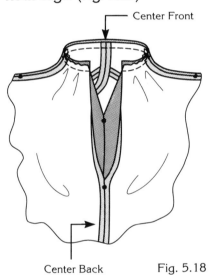

Center Back   Fig. 5.18

Turning the Pieces:

Turn the Ears rightside out.

Turn the bear to the rightside through the back opening. The arms and legs may be turned rightside out by pushing from the inside with your stuffing tool, starting at the tips of the paw and foot pads. Push the pads through the arms and legs to the outside.

If the machine stitching has trapped some fur in any seams, pull the pile to the rightside using the tip of a large needle.

Stuffing:

Work through the center back opening, and shape the pieces as you work. Refer to the general stuffing directions on page 15.

1. Stuff the head firmly. Pack the fiberfill tightly to fill out the muzzle and cheek areas. Add extra fiberfill at the back of the head and check the profile. You want the fiberfill to actually stretch the knit fur for a nice, full shape in back.

2. Insert enough fiberfill in the feet and hands to round out the shapes, but leave them medium-soft. Stuff the lower arms and lower legs loosely. Do not put any fiberfill between the elbow and shoulder or in the upper leg areas (the upper thigh), so that the limbs "flop" easily.

3. The body takes a moderate amount of stuffing. The bear's tummy should be soft, but the neck area of the body must be firm enough to support the head. Check that your bear sits properly, and adjust the stuffing if necessary. There should be enough fiberfill at the back opening so that you have to pull the edges tightly to make them meet.

Closing the Back Opening:

Use the 3-1/2" needle and a doubled length of carpet or upholstery thread for this hand stitching.

1. Form a secure knot in your thread, leaving a 6" tail on the knot. To reinforce the closure at the center back neck edge, insert your needle from the rightside, 1/4" in from the raw edges, just below the neck seam. Take a 1/4" vertical stitch

(going through the neck seam allowances). See Fig. 5.19.

2. From the rightside, insert your needle in the opposite side of the back opening, just above the neck seam. Take a 1/4" stitch on that side, also going through the neck seam allowances (Fig. 5.20).

3. Draw these two stitches together, poking the back seam allowances to the inside; tighten. Knot your thread to the 6" tail extending from your beginning stitch. Cut the threads about 2" from the bear and tuck the threads inside.

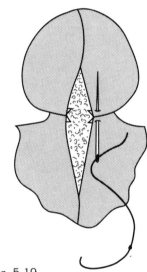

Fig. 5.19

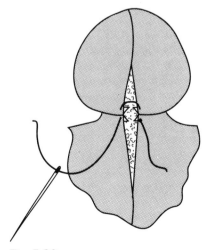

Fig. 5.20

4. Knot your thread again, this time at its end, and bring it up at the top of the center back opening. Working from the rightside of your material, close the entire opening using a hidden ladder stitch (page 18).

5. After your final knot, insert your needle into the bear, bringing it out a couple of inches away. Pull tightly and snip the thread right at the fabric backing. (This technique is shown on page 18.)

Sculpting the Face:

Use a very long, doubled length of heavy-duty thread and the 5" needle. Whenever you take a stitch on the rightside of the fur, use the tip of the needle to pull out any pile that might be trapped by the stitch. The pile should hide all your stitches.

1. Mark the mouth line with a quilting pin at each side. With a tape measure, find the location for the first pin by measuring 1-1/4" down from the bottom of the nose and 1/2" to the left of the center muzzle seam. Place the second pin 1/2" to the right of the seam. (The pins should be 1" apart, and correspond to points 3 & 4 in Fig. 5.21.)

2. Form a secure knot 6" from the ends of your thread. Referring to Fig. 5.21, insert your needle at the base of the muzzle, just below the chin dot (point 1). Bring the needle out at the inside corner of the eye (point 2).

3. Insert the needle close to the muzzle/face seam, taking a stitch less than 1/4" long. Bring the needle out at point 3. To begin shaping, push down on the eye with your thumb as you pull on the thread.

4. Take a 1" stitch, inserting your needle at point 4.

5. Bring the needle up at point 5, and take a stitch at the inside corner of this eye as you did with the first eye. Take a stitch inside the muzzle, coming out at point 4 again. Pull on your thread, pressing the eye down. The two corners of the mouth should begin to turn up, forming a smile.

6. You will strengthen your stitches by sewing a second set over them. As you work, continue to sculpt and shape the muzzle and the fiberfill. From point 4, insert your needle at point 3. Come out at point 2. Take a stitch at point 2; bring the needle out at point 3. Go in at point 4, and out at point 5. This time, after the short stitch at point 5, bring your needle out next to where you started (at point 1).

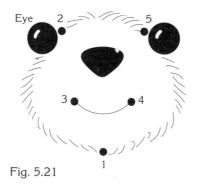

Fig. 5.21

7. When you are happy with your bear's expression, knot your thread to the 6" tail. Lose the ends of your working thread inside the head (page 18). Then thread the 6" tails on your shorter needle and hide them inside in the same manner.

Attaching the Ears:

1. Close the bottom of the ears with the hidden ladder stitch (page 18). Turn the raw edges to the inside as you work.

2. The ear placement affects the bear's expression, so pin the ears in several different locations on the head and decide where you want them. The ear wisps should be on the outer, bottom front of each ear. Mark your preferred location temporarily with quilting pins at the sides of each ear. For the top side of the ears on the Wispy you see here, measure down 2" on each side from the center top of the head. The top pins go in the Face piece, 1/2" in front of the side head seam. The bottom pins go on the seam line, 4" down from the center top of the head.

3. Sew the ears securely to the head, curving the tops of the ears forward to form a crescent shape. For extra safety, knot at both edges of the ears (because bears don't mind being picked up by their ears). Hide the ends of your threads inside the head. Remember to remove all the pins.

Eye Detail:

1. Visualize a horizontal line from the top of each eye to the muzzle. This forms a triangle of long pile between the eye and the muzzle, as in Fig. 5.22.

2. Carefully shorten the pile in this area to a length of 1/4" (or less, closer to the eye).

3. It is natural for the eye to be very close to the muzzle, and to have a little of the muzzle fur in front of the eye. But trim any other pile right next to the eyes (on the main Face piece) that may be covering the eye.

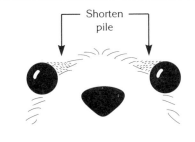

Fig. 5.22

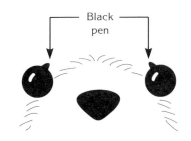

Fig. 5.23

4. With a black, permanent, fine-tipped pen, darken a spot of pile at the upper inside corner of each eye, as shown in Fig. 5.23.

Finishing Touches:

1. For child safety, don't tie a long ribbon around Wispy's neck. (See page 3.)

2. Give the entire bear a good brushing. Fluff the fur by brushing against the nap. Brush the back of the head and the back of the body down. If you understand Teddy Bear language, you just might catch your Wispy saying, "Thanks...I needed that!"

WISPY
Pattern
Layout

Nap
Direction ⟶

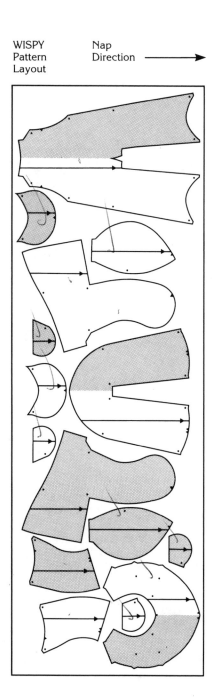

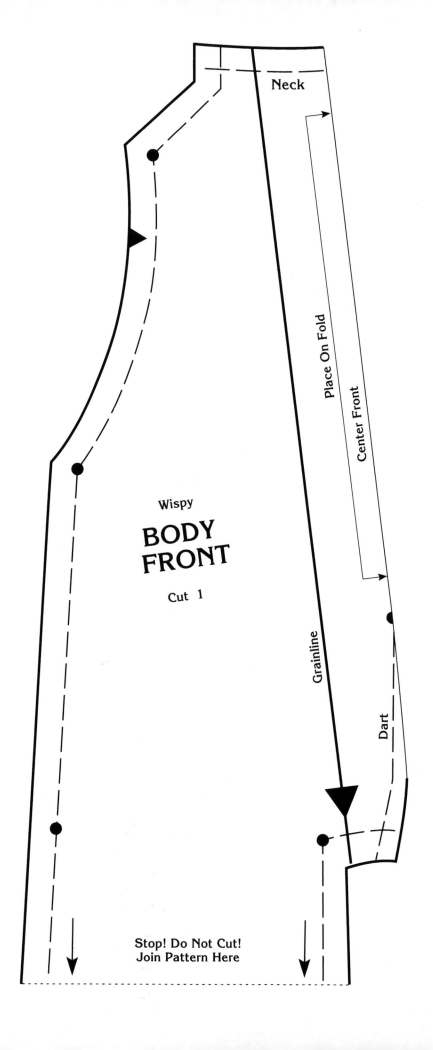

Neck

Place On Fold

Center Front

Wispy

BODY
FRONT

Cut 1

Grainline

Dart

Stop! Do Not Cut!
Join Pattern Here

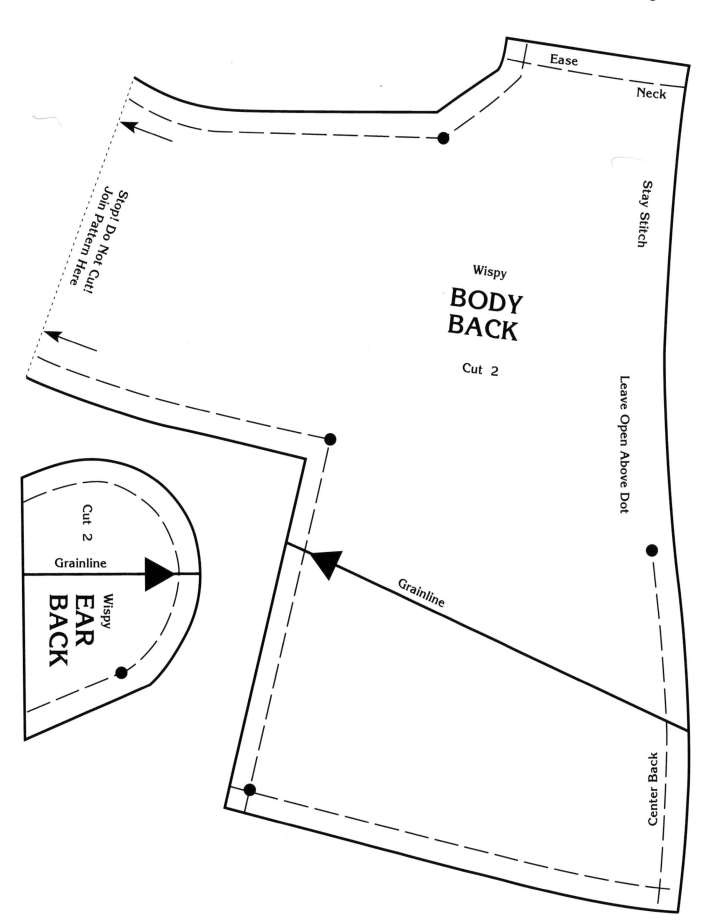

Ease

Neck

Stay Stitch

Leave Open Above Dot

Stop! Do Not Cut!
Join Pattern Here

Wispy

**BODY
BACK**

Cut 2

Cut 2

Grainline

Wispy

**EAR
BACK**

Grainline

Center Back

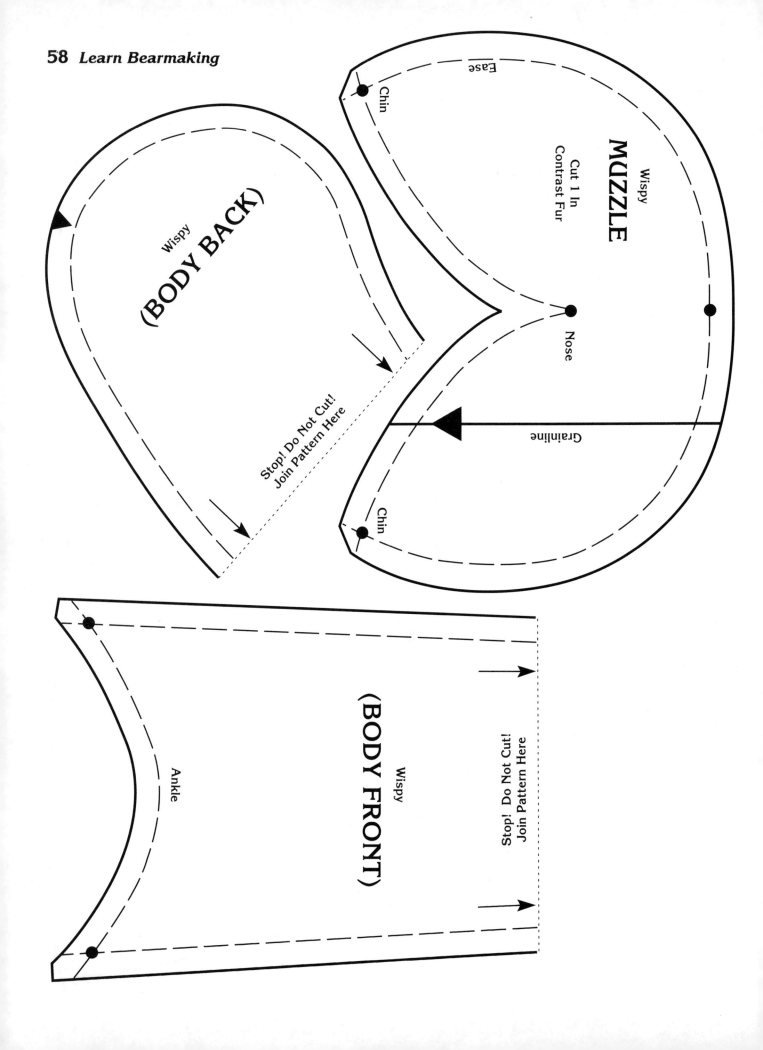

MUZZLE

Wispy

Cut 1 In
Contrast Fur

Ease

Chin

Nose

Grainline

Chin

Wispy

(BODY BACK)

Stop! Do Not Cut!
Join Pattern Here

Wispy

(BODY FRONT)

Ankle

Stop! Do Not Cut!
Join Pattern Here

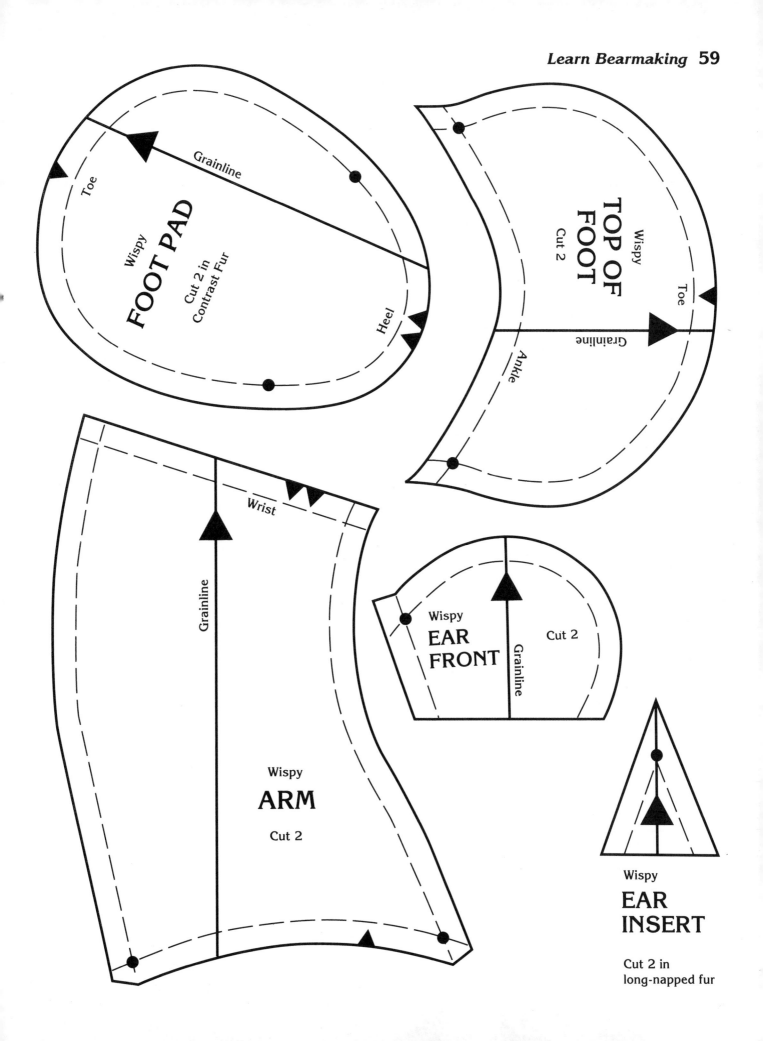

Wispy
FOOT PAD
Cut 2 in
Contrast Fur

Grainline

Toe

Heel

TOP OF FOOT
Cut 2
Wispy

Grainline

Toe

Ankle

Wrist

Grainline

Wispy
ARM
Cut 2

Wispy
EAR FRONT
Cut 2

Grainline

Wispy
EAR INSERT

Cut 2 in
long-napped fur

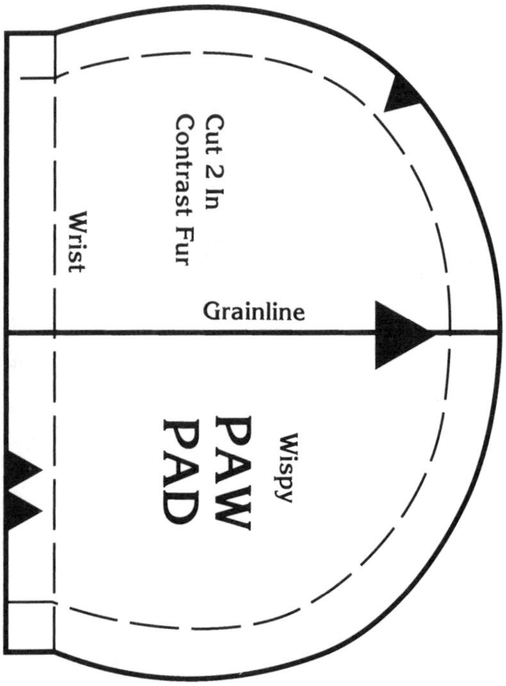

Cut 2 In
Contrast Fur

Wrist

Grainline

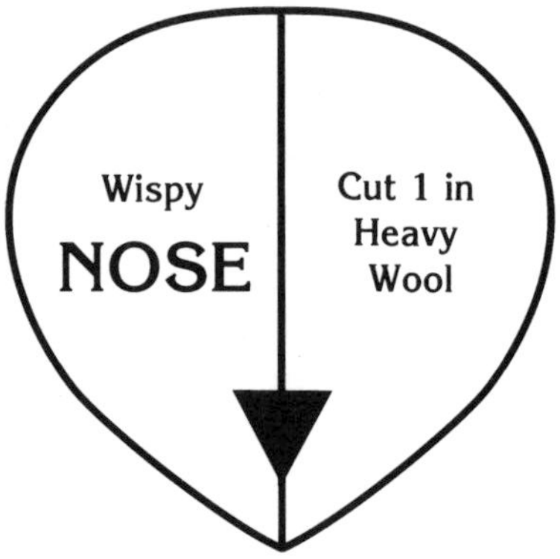

Wispy
**PAW
PAD**

Wispy
NOSE

Cut 1 in
Heavy
Wool

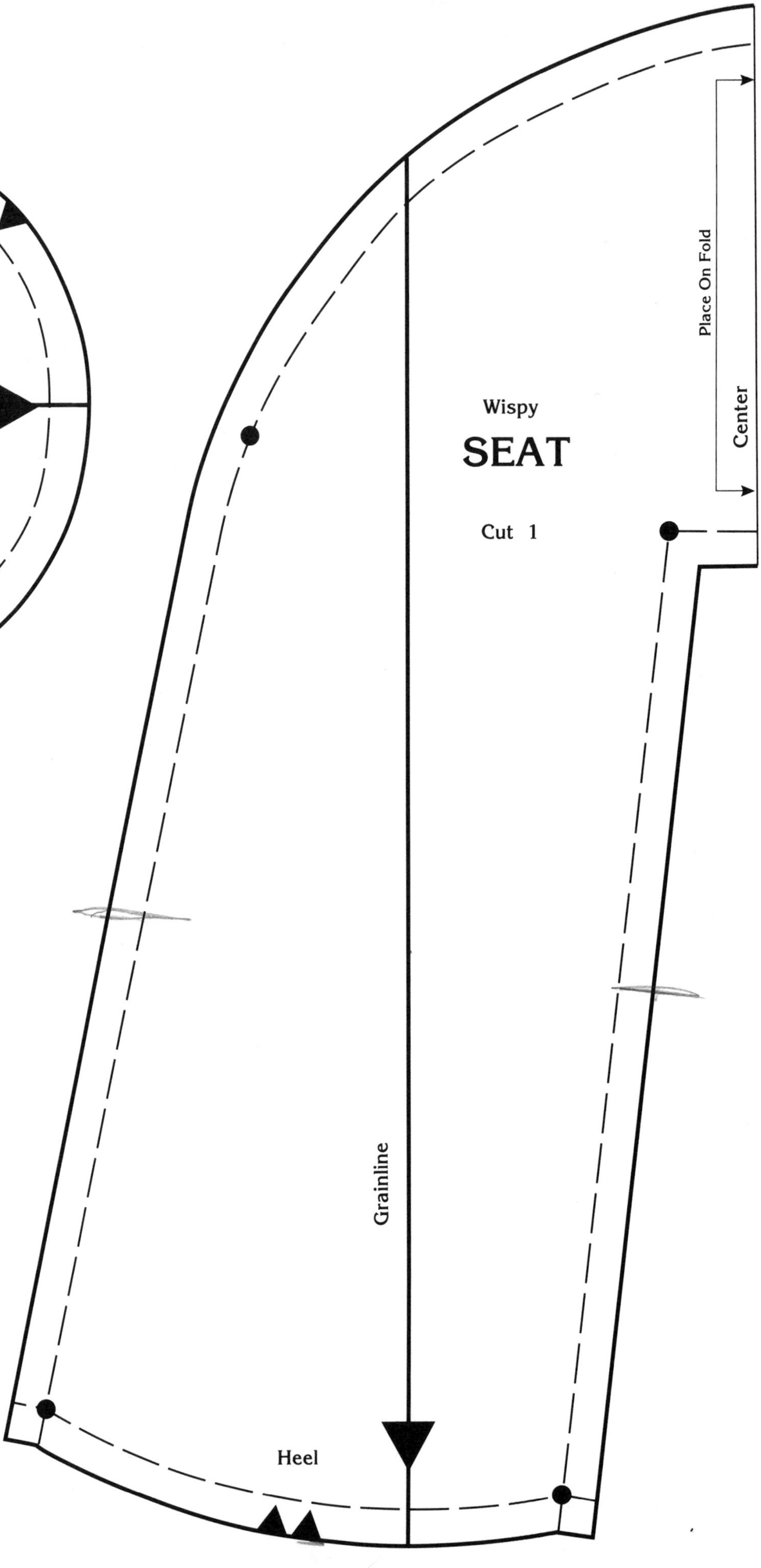

Wispy
SEAT

Cut 1

Place On Fold

Center

Grainline

Heel

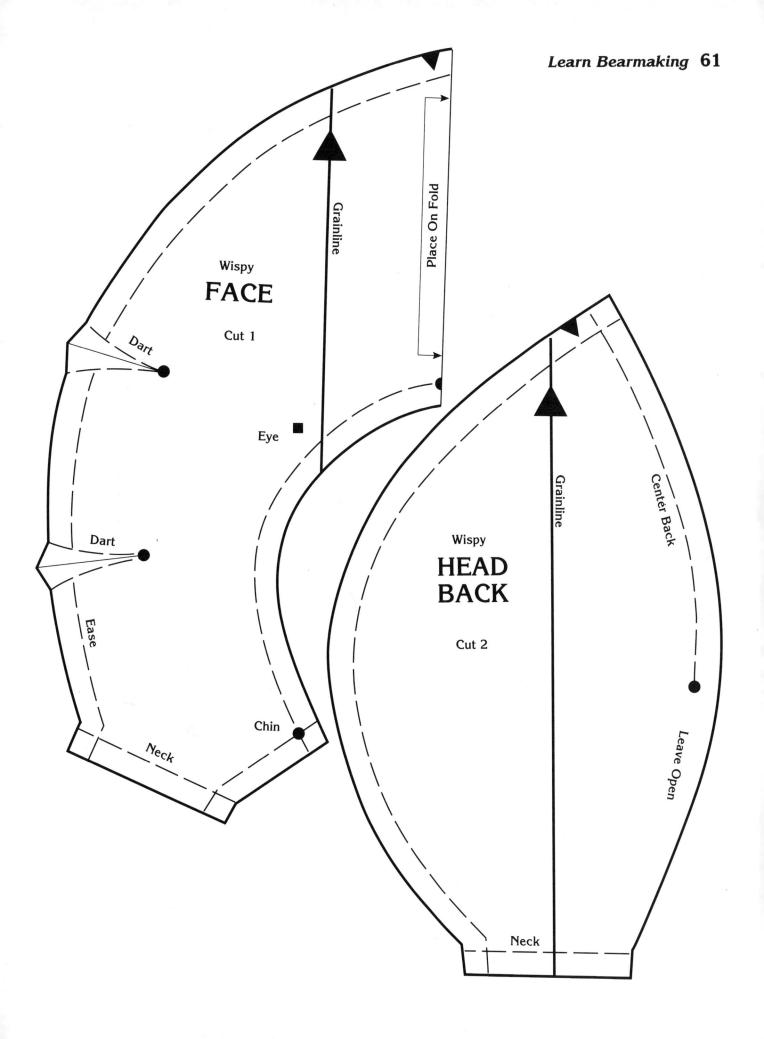

Wispy
FACE

Cut 1

Grainline

Place On Fold

Dart

Dart

Ease

Eye

Neck

Chin

Wispy
HEAD BACK

Cut 2

Grainline

Center Back

Leave Open

Neck

6. Bear On Course

Intermediate Techniques

All the intermediate and advanced bears in this book have one thing in common: they're jointed. This chapter will explain how to install two types of joints so that your bears can cock their heads or raise their arms or pose however they choose. We'll also cover the techniques you'll need to make either of the two intermediate patterns, Bearly Adequate or Cubby Cousins.

More Fur Factors

At this point, having mastered the easy patterns and the fundamentals, you are ready to delve into topics from Chapters 2 and 3 in more detail. Start by looking at more fur considerations (and you thought you already knew all about fur fabric).

Chapter 2 discussed how a fur's color affects a finished bear. The intermediate patterns feature muzzles and paw pads with shaved pile. Shortening the pile exposes the fur underneath, and that gives color a whole new dimension.

For example, a 1" knit fur often has a main pile and a shorter underfur. The underfur can be lighter, darker, or the same color as the main pile. See Figs. 6.1 and 6.2. The color of the underfur will affect the bear's expression where the pile is shortened for the muzzle.

Fig. 6.1 This cross section of a knit fur shows the 1-1/16" main pile and the shorter, dense underfur. The cream-colored underfur makes the shaved area slightly lighter than the blonde main fur.

Fig. 6.2 This variegated knit fur has a main pile composed of chocolate brown and tan fibers. The underfur is charcoal-almost black. Shaving the main pile reveals the darker fur underneath.

A second color modification occurs in variegated furs. These piles have two or more distinct shades of fibers mixed together (Fig. 6.3).

Manufacturers also manipulate color by tipping the ends of the main pile with a darker color (Fig. 6.4), or frosting with a lighter one (actually, lightening the main color with a bleach solution). For both tipped and frosted furs, the pile will change color when shaved.

A mill may use any combination of variegated pile, tipped or frosted pile, and contrasting underfur to produce distinctive fur fabrics. As you gain experience in bearmaking, you'll learn to predict how the placement of color in the pile will affect the finished bear.

Woven Synthetics

In addition to the variations discussed above, woven synthetics come either with guard hairs or level plush. Guard hairs are sparse fibers that extend beyond the main pile (Fig. 6.5). Occasionally you may find knit furs with guard hairs, but they are rare. Conversely, all the woven synthetics chosen for this book have guard hairs. They give the finished bear a luxurious appearance and a "fuzzy" feel.

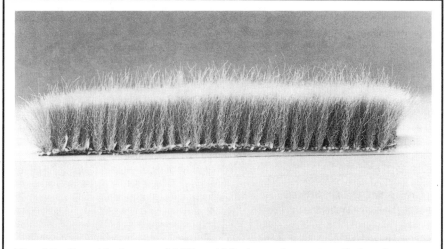

Fig. 6.5 Guard hairs stand 1/8" to 1/4" above the main pile height.

Fig. 6.3 A variegated pile has different colors of fibers. Each individual hair in the pile is a consistent color from its base to its tip. When shaved, the shortened pile matches the main fur.

Fig. 6.4 This fur has been tipped in a dark gray. The white pile underneath will show wherever the fur is shaved. (The Bearly Adequate behind the sewing machine on the front cover was constructed in this fur. Notice his lighter muzzle.)

Woven furs often require special handling to prevent raveling. Don't assume all woven furs will ravel, though, because some of the newer fabrics have a stabilized backing. There are two ways to detect a stabilized fur. First, you can feel the thin, rubbery coating on the backing, and second, it is more difficult to separate a single thread from the torn edge. Even though I prefer working with furs that have stabilized backings, I choose my fabric based on aesthetics rather than stabilizers.

The pattern pieces show where to leave the seams open for stuffing. If your fur ravels, you will need to finish these edges. For a fully jointed bear, six openings—twelve pieces—require special treatment.

After trimming the pile from the seam allowances (discussed below), but before seaming the pieces together, you may zigzag the opening edges by machine or overcast them by hand (Fig. 6.6). A quicker solution is to treat them with Fray Check™. Working from the wrongside, coat

the edges of the backing, staying within the seam allowances. Whichever method you choose, work an additional 1/2" beyond the openings' marks.

Woven furs are not always available, and the price per yard may be three or more times

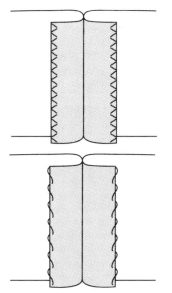

Fig. 6.6 Two methods to prevent raveling: zigzag by machine (top) or overcast by hand (bottom).

the cost of knits. Notwithstanding these drawbacks, some of the woven imported furs are outstanding choices for your teddy bear. If you want to use European furs and cannot find them in your area, check the Appendix. In addition, suppliers often advertise in teddy bear publications and exhibit at teddy bear shows. Most importers will send sample swatches for a nominal fee.

Shaving Pile

The color variations discussed above come into their own when shaving the pile for the bear's muzzle, paw pads or foot pads. For all fur types, pile shortening is identical.

Practice trimming on one of the fur scraps you saved from the pattern layout. Hold the shears horizontally, parallel to the fabric backing (Fig. 6.7). Trim the fur smooth, striving for a level surface. During this process, it helps to run the blunt edge of the shears against the nap to raise the

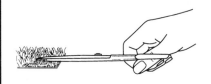

Fig. 6.7 Keep the blades of the shears parallel to the fur's backing when shortening the pile.

fibers. For extended contact, goggles and a face mask (Fig. 6.8) provide protection against airborne fibers.

View the fur from different angles while you work, especially from the side (Fig. 6.9). For 1" furs, shear off about 3/4", leaving a 1/4" plush. For furs with shorter naps, the trimmed pile should measure slightly less than half its original height.

This technique requires some patience and practice. And, like many other tasks, it requires sharp shears. (See page 103 for sharpening directions.)

Once you've finished trimming, take the pieces outdoors and shake out the loose fibers.

Electric dog clippers shave pile in no time flat. Hold the clippers the desired distance above the fur backing. A slow, steady movement will allow thick pile to feed into the cutting edge of the blades. The nap should run *toward* the clippers. If your family includes a poodle, you probably have electric clippers. Otherwise, they aren't worth the investment—unless you plan to go into teddy bear production.

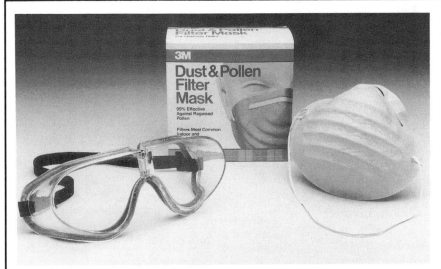

Fig. 6.8 For prolonged exposure, to avoid inhaling airborne fibers, wear a mask. Buy one suitable for pollens from a drugstore. It is more comfortable against your skin than the coarser ones from a hardware store. Use goggles to protect your eyes.

Fig. 6.9 The unattractive surface of this shortened pile needs additional work to clip it smooth.

Fig. 6.10 The seam allowances for the top seam were shaved before stitching. Compare the unshaved seam below it, which is much more conspicuous on the fur's rightside.

Concealed Seams

A related shaving technique may be applied to seam allowances. Trimming all the pile from the 1/4" seam allowances before stitching will result in nearly invisible seams (Fig. 6.10).

Snip the pile fibers right at the fabric backing on all seam allowances. Proper scissors will make this job easier (Fig. 6.11). Work near the edge of a table, holding the scissors flat against the tabletop. The handle of the scissors should be off the table to make room for your grip. While cutting, keep the scissors in the same position and slide the fabric to feed the pile into the blades. (Applique scissors have handles raised above the flat blades, so you do not need to work at the table edge.) Shake the trimmed pieces outdoors to rid them of loose fibers.

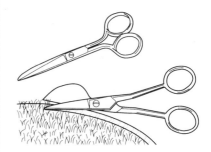

Fig. 6.11 Appropriate scissors ease shaving seam allowances. Try Gingher 6" duck-billed applique scissors or 5" sewing scissors.

Fig. 6.12 *The type of fur determines how noticeable the seams will be. Although neither of these bears has shaved seams, the pile on the right hides the seam lines better than the smooth pile on the left.*

Fig. 6.13 *The ear on the left (with shaved seam allowances) has a rounder shape than the flatter, untrimmed ear on the right.*

Trimming the seam-allowance pile is optional since it doesn't affect durability. Depending on the type of fur, you must decide if you want to trim (Fig. 6.12). For a typical jointed bear, this step may add 45 minutes or more to the construction time, but once you discern the difference, you might decide it's worth the extra effort.

If you don't want to shear all the seams, shave the seams in the critical areas. Specifically, the ear, paw pad, and head seams draw the most attention (Fig. 6.13).

Joints

So far, you've learned many criteria for judging quality in a handmade bear, such as superior materials, no fur trapped in seams, properly installed features, smooth stuffing, and invisible hand stitching. When it comes to jointed bears, though, quality means one more thing: tight joints.

Traditional bears often have wooden disks fastened with cotter pins. I don't recommend this jointing method, sometimes called "crown joints," because it requires strength and skill to capture the right tension.

However, if you have had past success with cotter pins and want to continue using them, Steve Schutt recommends the solid stainless steel variety rather than plated or aluminum types. Although more expensive, the solid stainless steel reliably holds its spring. Ask your hardware store to special order these cotter pins if it doesn't normally stock them.

I will discuss the two methods I prefer: plastic joints and bolts with locknuts. Try a sample joint first on scrap fur, before installing in your bear. If you've chosen plastic joints, purchase extra for your trial run because they are permanent; otherwise, to remove a plastic joint after installation, you must saw through the post with a hacksaw or nip it with heavy-duty wire cutters. Metal bolts with locknuts, on the other hand, may be removed from your scrap fabric and reused in your bear.

Plastic Joint Sets

Prepackaged plastic (nylon) joints offer the quickest solution. They come in sizes like 45mm, 55mm, and 65mm, which refer to the outside diameter of the disks. While plastic joints have the reputation of loosening over time, you can overcome this flaw with two strategies.

The first involves choosing the right type of joint. Regardless of the diameter of the joint disks, I recommend a thick post (Fig. 6.14). The preferred joint's post measures 5/16" in diameter, compared with 1/4" for the weaker post. The thicker assembly includes a larger washer with stronger locking capability.

The second safeguard against loosening is adding a metal lock washer. Unfortunately, plastic joints do not come packaged with these washers. You'll need size No. 5 (less than 3/4" outside diameter) metal lock washers for a joint with the smaller post. The larger post requires a size No. 7 (over 7/8" outside diameter). If you need only a few washers, a package of larger safety eyes with metal lock washers may cost less than the lock washers individually. Carver's Eye Co. (listed in the Appendix) sells both washer sizes in bulk.

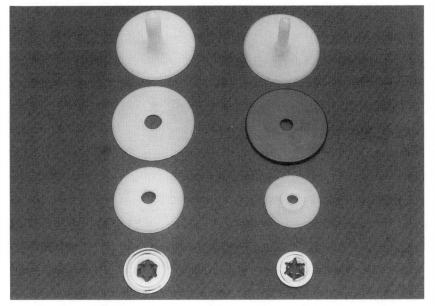

Fig. 6.14 A plastic joint with a wider post and larger washer will make a stronger, tighter joint. Although different manufacturers label both these joints "45mm," notice the difference in the post and lock washer sizes.

Plastic joint installation is simple:

1. Using an awl, poke holes where marked on the inner arms, inner legs, and body. If you've left gaps in the stitching lines, you won't need holes for the neck joint.

2. Enlarge the holes with a ball point pen or a special tool shown in Fig. 6.15. Try to separate the fabric threads without breaking them.

3. Insert the post piece of the joint into the arm, leg, or head and poke its shaft through the hole.

4. From the rightside, poke the shaft through the appropriate hole in the body.

5. Working through the body opening, place the flat disk on the shaft. The rounded edges go toward the fabric.

6. Snap the plastic lock washer onto the shaft with flat side down.

7. Using a wooden spool that fits over the shaft, force the washer down the shaft to tighten the joint. If you don't have a large spool, substitute a socket from a ratchet wrench set, and tighten the washer by hammering (Fig. 6.16).

8. Force a metal lock washer onto the shaft and tighten (Fig. 6.17).

Fig. 6.15 After poking a hole for the joint with an awl, enlarge it with the barrel of a ball point pen. Or, use an EasyGrip eye joint drill and a chopstick-tipped Stuffing Stick™ to enlarge it.

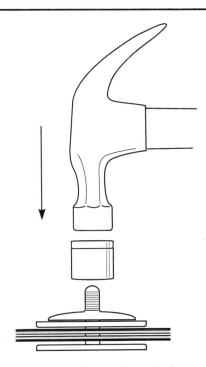

Fig. 6.16 Tighten plastic lock washers by hammering with a socket placed over the joint's shaft.

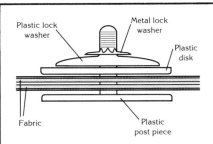

Fig. 6.17 To strengthen plastic joints, affix a metal lock washer—teeth up—on top of the plastic one.

Bolts and Locknuts

Another type of joint uses two hardboard disks fastened with a bolt and locknut (Fig. 6.18). Many professional teddy bear artists favor this hardy, durable jointing method. Sometimes suppliers sell these joints in sets of five (for one bear), but more often you pick out the individual components and assemble your own joints. Let's look at the hardware.

1. *Joint disks*: A number of manufacturers make disks in 1/8"-thick tempered hardboard. The disks are measured by diameter in inches, and are available in a wider selection of sizes than plastic joint sets. Sizes vary, depending on the supplier, with some disks ending up as much as 1/8" less than the labelled size. Besides the disk diameter, you have a choice of center hole sizes. Since you'll use 1/4" bolts, specify a 1/4" center hole. Note that hardboard washers shouldn't get wet—another reason not to throw your teddy in the washer. Each bear requires ten hardboard disks in the sizes indicated.

2. *Metal washers (10 required)*: Either of two sizes of metal washers may be used with the joint sets. The larger type, called fender washers, are 1-1/4" in diameter with a 1/4"

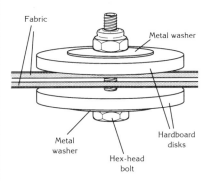

Fig. 6.18 Bolts, locknuts, metal washers, and hardboard disks make the strongest joint.

center hole. They produce the strongest joint because they reinforce more surface area on the hardboard washers. But they add weight to the bear. As an alternative, you may use standard metal washers. Instead of 1/4", I choose 5/16"

center holes because they have a larger outside diameter, almost 3/4". Although either fender or regular washers may be used for any of the jointed bears in this book, I use the standard washers for bears 13" or shorter, and the fender washers for taller bears.

3. *Bolts (5 required)*: Hardware stores handle a bewildering assortment of screws. The proper bin or box should be labeled 1/4" coarse, grade 5, plated, hex cap screws, with a large 1 (for 1" long).

4. *Locknuts (5 required)*: These metal locknuts, also called aero nuts, have locking nylon inserts. They are labeled 1/4" coarse, 20, plated, nylon locknuts.

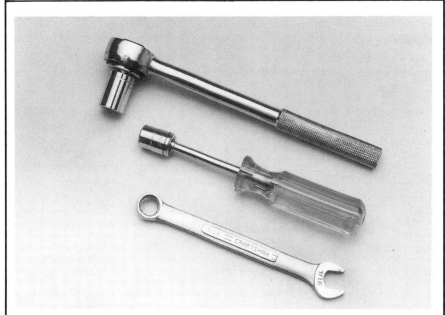

Fig. 6.19 Top to bottom: ratchet (socket) wrench, nutdriver, and a combination wrench that's both an open-end wrench and a box (closed-end) wrench.

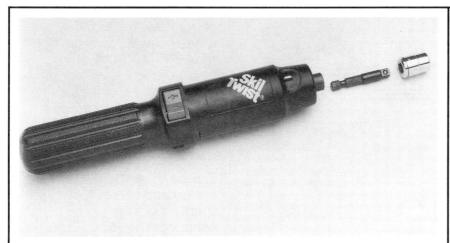

Fig. 6.20 A cordless screwdriver (optional) becomes a power nutdriver with the addition of a hex-to-square adapter to accommodate a 7/16" socket (both purchased separately).

5. *Tools*: You'll need two tools, one to hold the bolt and the other to tighten the locknut. You may use a nutdriver, a power nutdriver (optional), various wrenches, or a ratchet (socket) wrench for tightening (Figs. 6.19 and 6.20). The 7/16" size works for both the 1/4" hex cap screws and the locknuts.

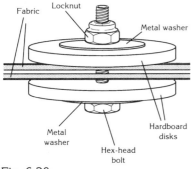

Fig. 6.20

Bolts, locknuts, metal washers, and wrenches are available in all hardware stores. Many of the suppliers in the Appendix carry hardboard disks.

To install a practice hardboard joint:

1. Poke and enlarge holes in a scrap of fur fabric as directed earlier for plastic joints.

2. Stack a metal washer and a hardboard disk on the 1" bolt.

3. Poke the bolt through the two layers of fabric, keeping the fur rightsides together.

4. Put the other hardboard disk and the second metal washer on the bolt.

5. Screw on the locknut with the wider part toward the disks and the narrower portion (with the nylon insert) facing away from the disks.

6. Tighten the locknut so that the joint feels tight but still moves. This step requires two tools: one to hold the bolt and the other to tighten the nut.

How much should you tighten it? Separate the two layers of fur and grasp the hardboard washers through the fur with both hands. Twisting your hands against each other, you should just be able to force the disks to turn. If you can't turn the joint, it's too tight; if it turns easily, it's too loose. The joint should start out very snug because the pile between the disks eventually mats down, causing the joint to loosen slightly. Some bearmakers avoid this problem by clipping all the pile that would have been between the two joint disks. I have not had any problems with the joints loosening, so I do not shave the pile covering the disks. If you are interested, Chapter 9 discusses an additional precaution against joints loosening.

When selecting the joint size for any teddy bear pattern, always use the largest disks possible, to assure a firm, secure joint. Additionally, don't limit yourself to one type of joint per bear. For example, you could decide on plastic joint sets for the shoulders and neck (for convenience, or to avoid extra weight), and bolts with locknuts for the hips (because legs have a wider range of movement).

Growlers

Adding a voice to a bear gives his personality an extra dimension. And it's easy.

Growlers come in different sizes, and the directions specify which fits best. But also consider that growlers come with different sounds, like a cow, a lamb, or a bear. Naturally, most teddy bear suppliers stock the ones with the bear voices, but I happen to love the large ones with a lamb sound. I think they make a grand teddy bear sound—younger and happier, like a playful cub. Many hobby shops carry them.

If your fiberfill breaks into small particles, cover the growler so that the fiberfill isn't sucked into it when it operates. For a simple growler covering, you can recycle clean pantyhose. Drop the growler into the toe and tie the stocking's foot with a wire twist tie, as used on food storage bags. Cut off the excess stocking about 1/2" from the tie (Fig. 6.21).

The growler's orientation inside the bear's tummy will determine how much movement it requires to growl. With a large growler and little extra room, you will have to position it with the holes facing up. This means the bear must be turned upside down in a

Fig. 6.21 For an easy growler cover, use nylons, knee-high stockings, or pantyhose. Tie the loose end with a twist tie.

Fig. 6.22 Orient the growler with the holes up or toward the front of the tummy.

headstand, and then righted again before he'll sound off. When possible, place the growler on an angle with the holes facing the front, letting the bear growl when tipped forward and then back. See Fig. 6.22.

For either orientation, place the perforated top of the growler as close as possible to the surface of the fur, while still maintaining a cushion of fiberfill between it and the fabric. Too much stuffing over the holes will mute the sound.

Now and then, a growler will fail for no apparent reason. When you've grown accustomed to hearing a bear, it's sad when he can't talk to you. Luckily, this problem only involves minor surgery to correct: snip the thread at the hand-closed back seam, remove the old growler, insert the new, and restitch the opening by hand.

So, when you make a teddy from the next two chapters, add a growler. Your grinning grizzlies will greet you with a grrrrowl.

7. Bearly Adequate

Fully Jointed Bear With Heart Pillow

Finished height: 17" (See color pages.)

When you're bearly adequate, you need extra love. This teddy doesn't have to worry about finding that extra love—he's irresistible. And when people hug him, they'll discover he's fully jointed: his arms, legs, and head swivel.

Over the years, this pattern has been the most popular of all my designs. Other bears may enjoy their own periods of popularity, but I keep coming back to this one. It was my first jointed design, and in it I tried to capture all that I associated with bears—"the essence of teddy bear."

They say a teddy bear reflects his or her maker. I see a little insecurity in the expression of my Bearly Adequate bears, not evident in my later patterns. (After the success of this design, I had more confidence, and the bears show it.) It's precisely that insecurity that gives this bear an endearing quality. He remains one of my favorites.

Don't be afraid of making a jointed bear—it's easy. And Bearly Adequate is an excellent choice for your first attempt. The pattern pieces are large, and the long pile requires less construction precision than a short-pile fur. The directions assume you have already read Chapters 2, 3, and 6.

Fur Selection Guide:

This pattern was designed for the domestic fur that many fabric shops stock specifically for bearmaking. It should have a pliable knit backing, and a dense 15/16" to 1-1/16" pile. Often these furs are variegated, or they have a different shade of underfur. I've made Bearly Adequate in eleven different colors, from pure white to charcoal, and all the natural beiges and browns in between. All of them made charming bears, so you have a lot of freedom selecting a color.

Also, consider the appropriate foot-pad treatment:

- Shaved foot pads and paw pads: This works for any fur with a dense underfur, and is especially nice when the underfur contrasts with the main pile.

- Tinted toe-pad detail: Since a black, permanent marking pen is used for tinting, this technique looks best on medium to dark furs.

- Natural, untrimmed pile: This is the easiest choice, of course, for any fur. The finished bear will still have a soft, warm appeal.

Materials:

3/8 yd knit fur fabric (60" wide), 15/16" to 1-1/16" pile height

Small piece of black coat wool

Two 15mm black eyes and their lock washers

One 18mm eye and lock washer

Small piece of strong, flexible plastic (such as a coffee can lid)

Black perle cotton No. 3—thick (optional)

Polyester fiberfill

One 65mm (2-1/2") joint set

Four 55mm (2") joint sets

One 2-3/8" growler (optional)

Nylon stocking to cover growler (optional)

Pattern Pieces:

Make a full set of 11 pattern templates from the patterns on pages 86-89.

Cutting Directions: *Follow the fur layout diagram.*

Cut one Muzzle and one Face. Cut two each of Body Front, Body Back, Head Back, and Foot Pads. Cut four each of Arms, Legs, and Ears. You should have a total of 22 fur pieces. Transfer all pattern markings to the wrongside.

Trimming the Pile:

From the rightside, holding scissors flat against the backing, trim the pile from all seam allowances.

Shaving the Muzzle:

Using a scrap of fur, practice trimming the pile to a height of 1/4". (The previous chapter explains how.) Once you have mastered the technique, trim the pile on the entire muzzle to 1/4".

Shaving the Pads (Optional):

If you have decided to use the shaved pad treatment, trim the pile on the Foot Pads to a height of 1/4". For the paw pads, notice that the Arm has a trim line marked on it. Shave the pile to a height of 1/4" up to this line on the inside Arms only. You need one left and one right Arm; they will be mirror images of each other. Do not trim any pile on the other two Arm pieces (the outside Arms).

First Pinning:

1. Pin two Ear pieces together along the curved edges, leaving bottom edges open. Repeat for the other ear. (Fig. 7.2)

2. Pin two Arm pieces together, leaving open between dots. (Note: If you have shaved the paw pads, make sure you match up one inner arm and one outer arm.) Repeat for the other arm. (Fig. 7.3)

3. Pin two Leg pieces together, leaving open between dots. Also, leave the bottom of the Leg open for the Foot Pad. Repeat for the other leg. (Fig. 7.4)

4. Pin the Head Backs together along the center back seam, leaving open between dots. (Fig. 7.5)

5. Pin the Body Fronts together along the center front, matching the double notches. (Fig. 7.6)

6. Pin the Body Backs together along the center back, leaving open between dots. (Fig. 7.7)

Fig. 7.2

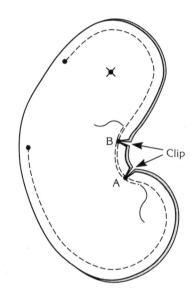

Fig. 7.3

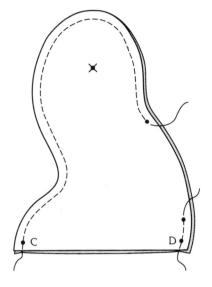

Fig. 7.4

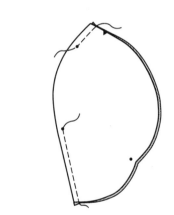

Fig. 7.5

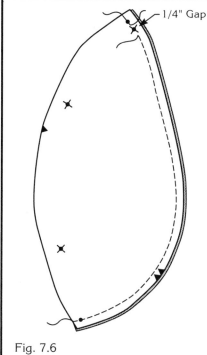

1/4" Gap

Fig. 7.6

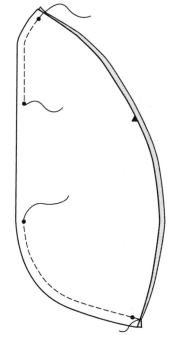

Fig. 7.7

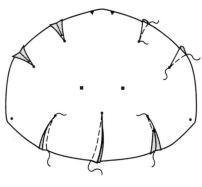

Fig. 7.8

First Stitching: *All seam allowances are 1/4".*

1. Stitch two Ear pieces together along the curved edges, leaving the straight bottom edge open. Repeat for other ear. (Fig. 7.2)

2. Sew two Arm pieces together, leaving open between the dots for turning. To reinforce the inner curve, stitch again over the first stitching. Clip the seam allowance to the seam line at points "A" and "B." Repeat for the other arm. (Fig. 7.3)

3. Stitch two Leg sections from point "C" to dot. Stitch from the other dot to point "D." (Fig. 7.4)

4. Stitch the center back seam of the head, leaving open between the dots. (Fig. 7.5)

5. Sew the center front body seam, leaving a 1/4" gap in the seam at the "X" for the neck joint. (Fig. 7.6)

6. Sew the center back body seam, leaving open between dots. (Fig. 7.7)

7. Make seven darts in the Face. Slit the top four darts. Open these darts and clip all pile from the seam allowances. Pull this loose pile out of the stitching lines to avoid depressions on the rightside. (Fig. 7.8)

Installing the Eyes:

To install the 15mm eyes, follow the directions on page 21.

Second Pinning:

1. Pin a Foot Pad into the bottom opening of a leg, having the raw edges even and matching points "C" and "D." Pin with the Foot Pad facing you, easing it to fit. Repeat for the other leg. (Fig. 7.9)

2. Pin the Body Front to the Body Back all the way around the side seams, matching notches and dots. (Fig. 7.10)

3. Pin the Face to the Head Backs, matching the notches and center top of the head. Pin from one point "E," around the top of the head, to the other "E," leaving the neck edge open. (Fig. 7.11)

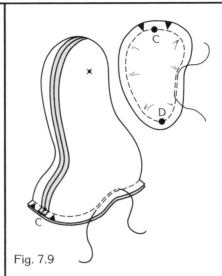

Fig. 7.9

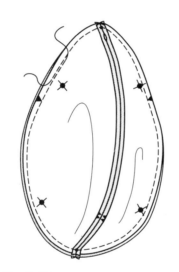

Fig. 7.10

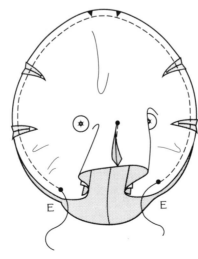

Fig. 7.11

Second Stitching:

1. With the Foot Pads down, carefully stitch the Foot Pads to the legs, removing pins as you come to them. (Fig. 7.9)

2. Seam the Body Front to the Body Back at side seams. (Fig. 7.10)

3. Seam the Face to the Head Backs by stitching around the top of the head, from one point "E" to the other. (Fig. 7.11)

Finishing the Ears:

Turn the ears rightside out. Sew the bottom of the ears closed with a hidden ladder stitch, turning the raw edges to the inside along the seam line. To form a depression in the ear front, trim the pile to a height of 1/4" on the center area inside the dotted line on the pattern. (For hints on trimming pile, see Chapter 6.)

Preparing the Body:

Using an awl, make holes at the "X's" for the joints. If threads of the material are broken by the awl, reinforce the fabric on the wrongside with circles of glue around these holes. Let the glue dry.

Jointing the Head:

1. Working on the Face piece only (not the Head Backs) with a doubled length of upholstery thread, gather the bottom edge of the Face by hand with a running stitch from one point "E" to the other "E." Pull the thread tightly and knot (but do not cut) your thread. (Fig. 7.12)

2. Pin the back neck edge to these gathers, making a tuck at each side of the Head Backs. With a backstitch, hand sew the back neck edges to the front gathered edge. As you work, knot your stitching in the middle of this seam (at both sides of the face's center dart), leaving a small gap at the dart for jointing. (Fig. 7.13)

3. Turn the head and the body rightside out. Install the 65mm (2-1/2") neck joint following the directions in Chapter 6.

Stuffing the Head:

Pay particular attention to the shape of the head. The neck edges have both darts and gathers, providing a lot of full-ness. Pack extra fiberfill into the lower face to fill out this fabric. The cheeks should be plump. The center of the face should be somewhat flatter than the sides because the muzzle will nestle between the cheeks.

Making the Nose:

Cut one Nose Base from the flexible plastic. Punch a hole in the center of the Nose Base with a 1/8" hole punch. Enlarge the hole by punching it several times, slightly offset each time, so that the shank of the eye fits through it easily. (Or, using a wood backup, drill a hole with an electric or hand drill and a 5/32" bit.) Poke the shank of the extra eye through the hole.

Cut one Nose from the wool. With upholstery thread, make a running stitch along the raw edges of the Nose to gather. Partially tighten the gathers.

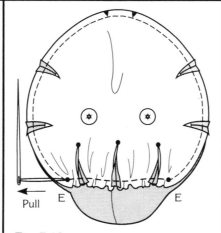

Fig. 7.12

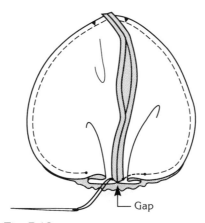

Fig. 7.13

Fig. 7.14

Stuff the Nose lightly with fiber-fill. Place the 18mm eye with the plastic Nose Base on the stuffing. The shank of the eye will extend out the back of the nose. Pull up the gathers to close tightly over the base.

Knot your thread and make several crossing stitches over the gathers. The size of the nose is determined by the amount of stuffing and how tightly the gathers are pulled. For a younger-looking bear, make a smaller nose.

Poke a hole where indicated on the Muzzle. Trim all pile (down to the backing) from the area that will be covered by the nose. Insert the nose shank into the hole on the Muzzle, and glue the nose wool to the Muzzle. Attach a metal lock washer to the shank; press a wooden spool down the shank to tighten.

Gathering the Muzzle

Using a doubled length of upholstery thread, gather the outer edge of the Muzzle by hand with a running stitch. Pull the gathers partially closed. Stuff the Muzzle, then pull the gathers tight, and knot. Further close this opening with several crossing stitches over the gathers. Flatten the gathers at the back so that the Muzzle forms a half ball (Fig. 7.14). Measure the Muzzle with a tape measure, without flattening the pile. The circumference should be about 8-1/2" for an adult bear. Smaller muzzles, about 8", give the impression of a younger bear. Muzzle size may be reduced by trimming the pile shorter.

Sculpting the Mouth:

Temporarily place four quilting pins corresponding to Fig. 7.15. Using two strands of upholstery thread, knot the thread on the back of the muzzle and bring your needle up at the pin at point 1. Insert the needle at point 2 and come out at 3, catching the thread (Fig. 7.16). Insert the needle at 4 and pull it through to the back of the muzzle. Tighten the stitches to shape the mouth; knot. If desired, repeat these steps using two strands of black perle cotton over the upholstery thread stitches. Trim the pile along the thread lines to emphasize mouth shaping (Fig. 7.17). Also, trim the muzzle pile above the nose to flatten it for the bridge of the nose (the area that will be between the eyes).

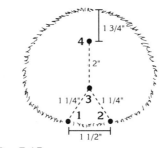

Fig. 7.15

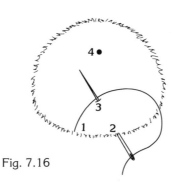

Fig. 7.16

Fig. 7.17

Attaching the Features:

Pin the muzzle and ears to the face and experiment with different placements. Once you have decided where to place them, mark the locations by putting pins into the head at the top and bottom of each ear and all the way around the muzzle. (Fig. 7.18)

On the face, trim any pile that will be under the muzzle (Fig. 7.19). Additionally, trim remaining pile from the back of the muzzle. With a long, doubled length of upholstery thread and a 5" needle, anchor the muzzle to the face by taking four stitches, one each at the top, bottom, and both sides of the muzzle. Next, work around the entire muzzle with a backstitch: take a 1/2" stitch forward through the face, and then stitch backwards 1/4" through the muzzle. Pull the thread taut and knot it several times while stitching. End off and hide the thread tails inside.

Thread a 7" needle with a long, double strand of upholstery thread and tie a large knot about 6" from the end (see Fig. 7.18).

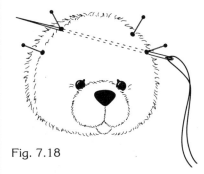

Fig. 7.18

From the rightside, insert the needle at the bottom of the left ear and bring out at the top of the right ear. Guide the needle with your hand through back head opening if your needle is too short. Taking a 1/4" stitch, insert the needle and bring out at the top of the left ear. Take a 1/4" stitch and bring the thread out at the bottom of the right ear. Take a 1/4" stitch, bringing the thread out next to your beginning knot. To form depressions for the ears, shape the head by tightening the thread and knotting it to the loose

Fig. 7.19

ends. Hide the ends inside the head, thread your needle with the 6" tails, and hide them inside also.

Sew the head opening closed with a hidden ladder stitch. Sew the ears securely in place, knotting at both sides of each ear. Remove all pins.

Jointing the Arms and Legs:

On the inside only of each arm, poke a hole at the "X" with an awl for the joint, making sure there is one left and one right arm. (Note: If you shaved the inside arms for paw pads, poke holes in those

pieces, not in the outside arms.) Turn rightside out.

Notice the difference between the right and left legs. The arch of the Foot Pad goes toward the inside. On the inside only of each leg: poke a hole at the "X" with an awl for the joint. Make certain you end up with a right and a left leg. (The bear will look pretty funny if you don't.) Turn rightside out.

Joint the arms and legs according to the directions starting on page 68.

Stuffing:

While this bear should be stuffed firmly to support tight joints, the center of his tummy may be stuffed softer. If you're using a growler, see page 71. When stuffing the legs, maintain the arch in the foot. As you stuff the arms, curve them in toward the tummy.

Check that your bear is smooth all over, especially around the joint disks. If necessary, adjust the fiberfill so that your bear sits squarely. Bearly Adequate should also stand on his own, albeit somewhat precariously. Once you are satisfied with the stuffing job, close the openings of the arms, legs, and body with the hidden ladder stitch.

Tinting the Foot Pads (Optional):

Practice this technique on a fur scrap before trying it on a finished bear. Pin the completed sample over the bear's foot to preview the effect. To help you visualize what to trim on the bear, cut scraps of fabric and temporarily pin them in place: using Fig. 7.20 as a guide, cut three Toes and a Ball of the Foot from a scrap of fabric (preferably black felt or coat wool, but almost any material will do). Temporarily pin these pieces on the stuffed foot pad. The large toe goes over the arch of the foot and the smaller toe is outside. Once properly placed, remove the fabric and trim the pile

under these guides to a height of 1/4". Using a black, felt-tipped marker (that specifies permanent on cloth), darken the 1/4" pile to define the toes and the ball of the foot.

Detailing the Eye:

Trim the pile above the inside corners of the eyes (Fig. 7.21). Also trim any fur covering the eye. Using a permanent black marking pen, darken the fur as in Fig. 7.22 for light furs. For dark furs, color the areas in Fig. 7.23. (Timid? Poke an extra eye through a fur scrap, and practice.)

Follow Fig. 7.24 for brushing the finished bear.

Ball of Foot

Toe

Toe

Large Toe

Arch

Actual Size

Fig. 7.20

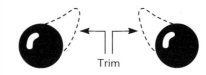

Trim

Fig. 7.21

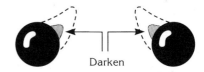

Darken

Fig. 7.22

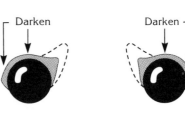

Darken

Darken

Fig. 7.23

Fig. 7.24 *1. Using a stiff bristled brush, gently brush the finished bear. Brush the face in the direction indicated by the arrows. 2. With your fingertip, pull expression lines up from the inside corners of the eyes toward the center forehead.*

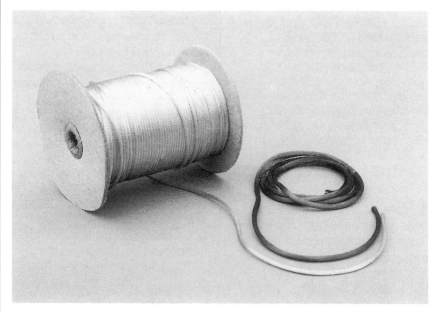

Fig. 7.25 *Rattail cord comes in two thicknesses on spools, and is usually sold by the yard at craft and hobby shops. Either thickness will work.*

Heart Pillow

Many teddy bear enthusiasts insist that all teddy bears talk...but not all humans hear them. Whether or not your bear talks, make sure he gets his point across by stitching a heart with his own message. Choose from a variety of sayings or stitch a tiny portrait of Bearly Adequate holding his own heart that reads, "You are loved beary much."

Materials:

For the sayings on page 85: 6" square of 14 count Aida

For the bear holding the heart motif (page 84): 6" square of 22 count Hardanger

6" square of velour fabric for backing (another square of Aida or Hardanger may be substituted for velour)

1/2 yd ruffled eyelet trim about 1" wide (match the color of your evenweave fabric)

1/2 yd rattail trim or other decorative cord with a diameter of 1/8" or less (See Figs. 7.25 and 7.26.)

2/3 yd picot-edged ribbon 1/2" wide

Small artificial flower or holly sprig

Small amount of polyester fiberfill

Sewing thread

Elastic thread (optional)

White glue

Pillow Directions:

1. Following the counted cross stitch directions in Chapter 4, center and stitch your chosen design on the 6" square of evenweave fabric.

2. For the bear holding the heart (page 84):

(a) Complete the solid area of DMC 754 before backstitching the words on top.

(b) Practice the eyes and nose on a scrap of evenweave fabric. The eyes and nose are satin stitched over the completed face with one strand of black. Just cross stitch a small area in DMC 738. Try satin stitching with a fine needle rather than the tapestry needle. Start with a stitch in the middle of the eye or nose. Satin stitch to one edge of the solid black area, then return to the center and work to the other edge. The eyelash is a single straight stitch. Add a tiny stitch of white (one strand) on top of the finished eye for highlight. Make several eyes and noses over these cross stitches, and choose your favorite expression.

3. After completing the embroidery, block it. (See Glossary.)

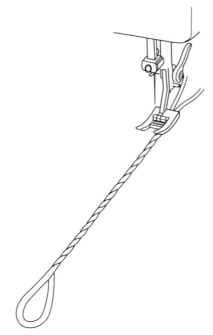

Fig. 7.26 Twist 6-strand embroidery floss to make a decorative cord. Start with floss about five times the desired length. Fold it in half, and secure one doubled end temporarily under your sewing machine's presser foot. Twist the doubled floss very tightly. Hold it in the middle, bring the two ends together (keeping the thread taut), and then let go of the middle. The two halves will twist against each other, forming a single cord.

4. Make a template from the heart pattern on page 83. Place the template over the embroidery, matching centers and aligning the arrows with the weave of the fabric. Trace around the template with a pencil. Cut on pencil line.

5. Cut another pattern piece in velour (or plain evenweave fabric) for the backing. The pattern includes a 1/4" seam allowance.

6. Pin the ruffled eyelet trim around the embroidered pillow front, rightsides together. The bound edge of the eyelet should be even with the raw edges of the fabric. The ruffle extends toward the center of the heart. Begin and end the eyelet at the "X." Ease extra trim around the curves. Pleat the eyelet at the bottom of the heart, adding about 1" extra at that point. Overlap the eyelet ends at the "X" and cut off any extra trim.

7. Stitch the eyelet to the pillow front on the seam line.

8. With rightsides together, pin the heart front to the backing piece, sandwiching the eyelet between the two pattern pieces. Stitch, using your prior stitching line as a guide, leaving open between the dots. Be careful not to catch the ruffle in the seam. To reinforce at the top center, stitch again over your first stitching.

9. Clip curves, and trim the seam allowance at the bottom point. Clip the top center to the dot. Grade seams; turn to rightside.

10. Stuff evenly with fiberfill. Sew the opening closed by hand.

11. Beginning at the bottom, glue or sew rattail cord at the base of the eyelet, on the fabric seam line (Fig. 7.27). Cut off any excess cord.

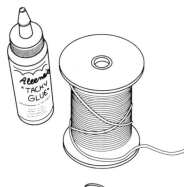

Fig. 7.27 Apply a very thin bead of glue along the seam line. A glue applicator will give you more control than the bottle's tip. Twist the rattail cord and press it into the glue.

12. Loop the ribbon as shown in Fig. 7.28. Wind a piece of 6-strand embroidery floss around the center of the bow; knot. Attach the flower or holly to the bow with the floss. Knot at the back and snip the thread

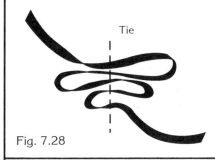

Tie

Fig. 7.28

ends. Cut the ends of the ribbon at an angle. (Note that the small flower makes this accessory inappropriate for young children.)

13. Glue or sew the bow to the bottom point of the pillow.

14. To make it easier for your teddy bear to hold his new pillow, cut elastic thread to fit around one or both of your bear's paws. String the elastic through a hole in the eyelet, and knot. The elastic loop(s) will be hidden under the bear's fur.

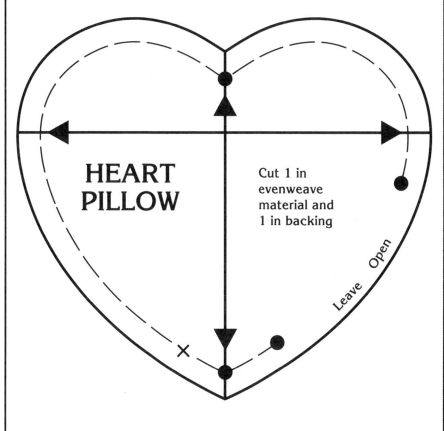

HEART PILLOW

Cut 1 in evenweave material and 1 in backing

Leave Open

BEARLY
ADEQUATE
Pattern
Layout
3/8 yd
snug fit

Nap
Direction

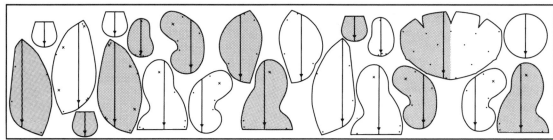

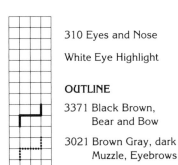

Stitch Count: 38 high by 49 wide

KEY	DMC COLOR NUMBER
∩ ∩	436 Tan
✕ ✕	434 Brown, light
• •	738 Tan, very light
– –	739 Tan, ultra very light
∨ ∨	519 Sky Blue
▲ ▲	518 Wedgewood, light
△ △	754 Peach Flesh, light
⁄ ⁄	353 Peach Flesh

310 Eyes and Nose

White Eye Highlight

OUTLINE

3371 Black Brown,
Bear and Bow

3021 Brown Gray, dark
Muzzle, Eyebrows

355 Terra Cotta, dark
Heart and Words

Threads per inch of fabric	Finished design size in inches
Hardanger 22	1-3/4 by 2-1/4
Aida 18	2-1/8 by 2-3/4
Aida 14	2-3/4 by 3-1/2
Aida 11	3-1/2 by 4-1/2

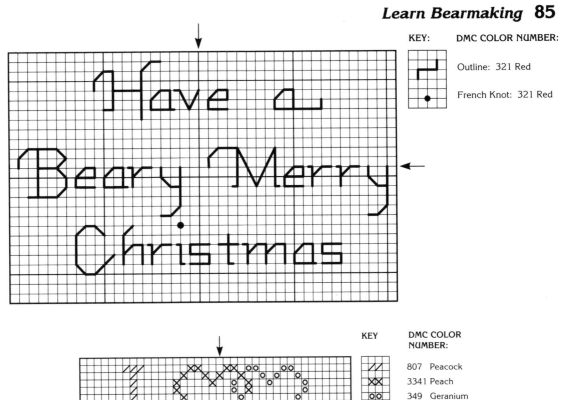

KEY:	DMC COLOR NUMBER:

Outline: 321 Red

French Knot: 321 Red

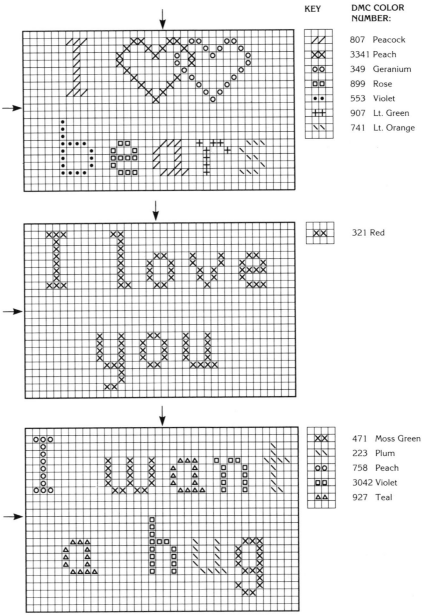

KEY	DMC COLOR NUMBER:
⌗	807 Peacock
XX	3341 Peach
OO	349 Geranium
□□	899 Rose
••	553 Violet
++	907 Lt. Green
\\	741 Lt. Orange

XX	321 Red

XX	471 Moss Green
\\	223 Plum
OO	758 Peach
□□	3042 Violet
△△	927 Teal

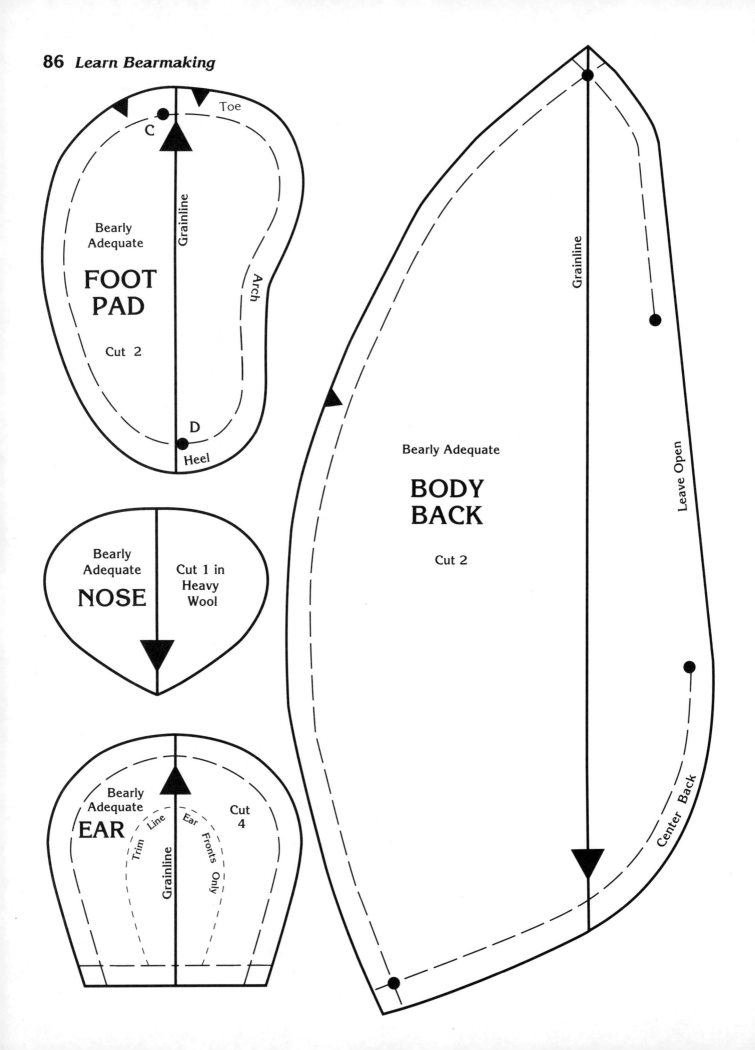

Toe

C

**Bearly
Adequate**

Grainline

Arch

**FOOT
PAD**

Cut 2

D

Heel

**Bearly
Adequate**

NOSE

Cut 1 in
Heavy
Wool

**Bearly
Adequate**

EAR

Trim Line

Ear Fronts Only

Grainline

Cut 4

Bearly Adequate

**BODY
BACK**

Cut 2

Grainline

Leave Open

Center Back

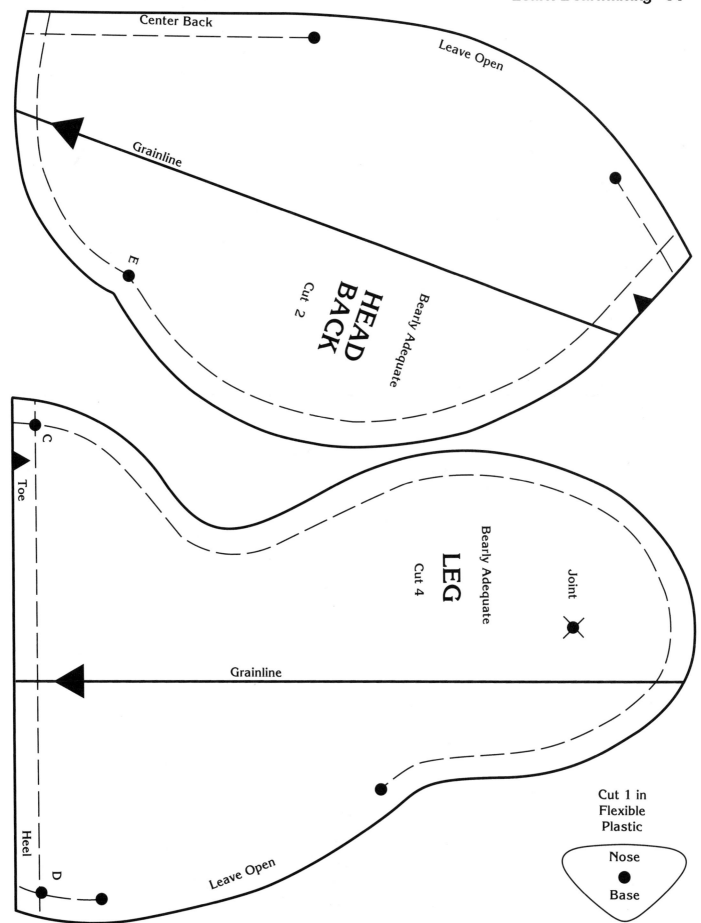

Center Back

Leave Open

Grainline

E

HEAD BACK
Cut 2

Bearly Adequate

C

Toe

Grainline

LEG
Cut 4

Bearly Adequate

Joint

Heel

D

Leave Open

Cut 1 in
Flexible
Plastic

**Nose
Base**

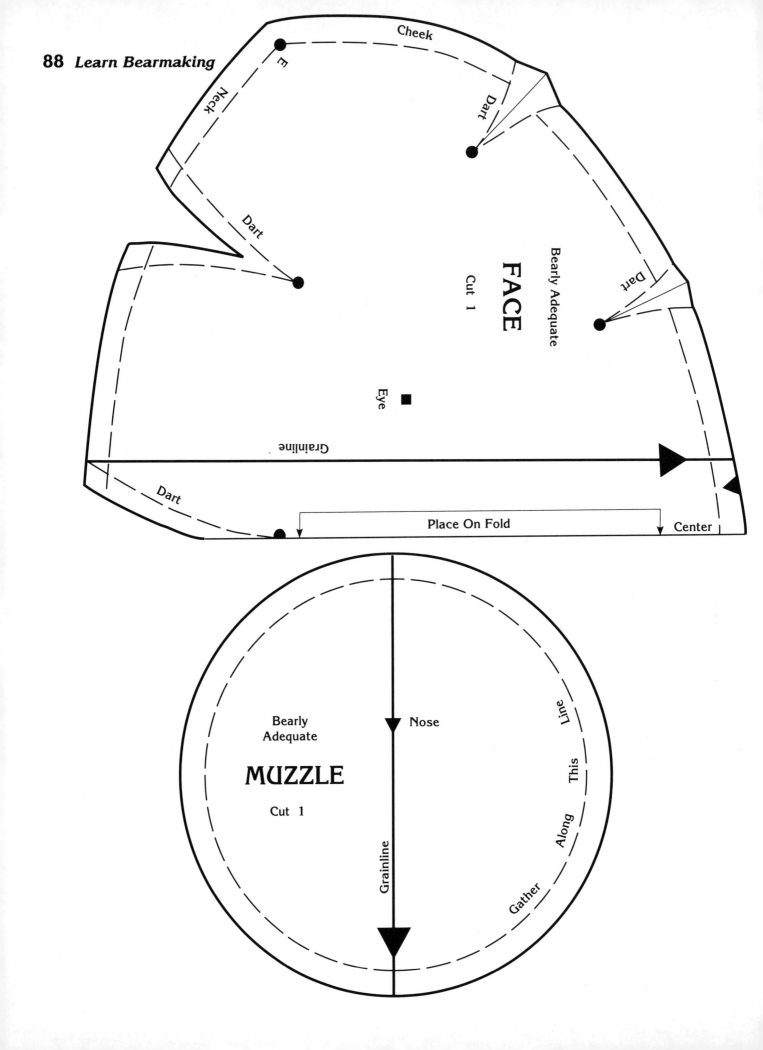

Cheek

Neck

E

Dart

Dart

Bearly Adequate

FACE

Cut 1

Dart

Eye ■

Grainline

Dart

Place On Fold

Center

Bearly
Adequate

MUZZLE

Cut 1

Nose

Gather Along This Line

Grainline

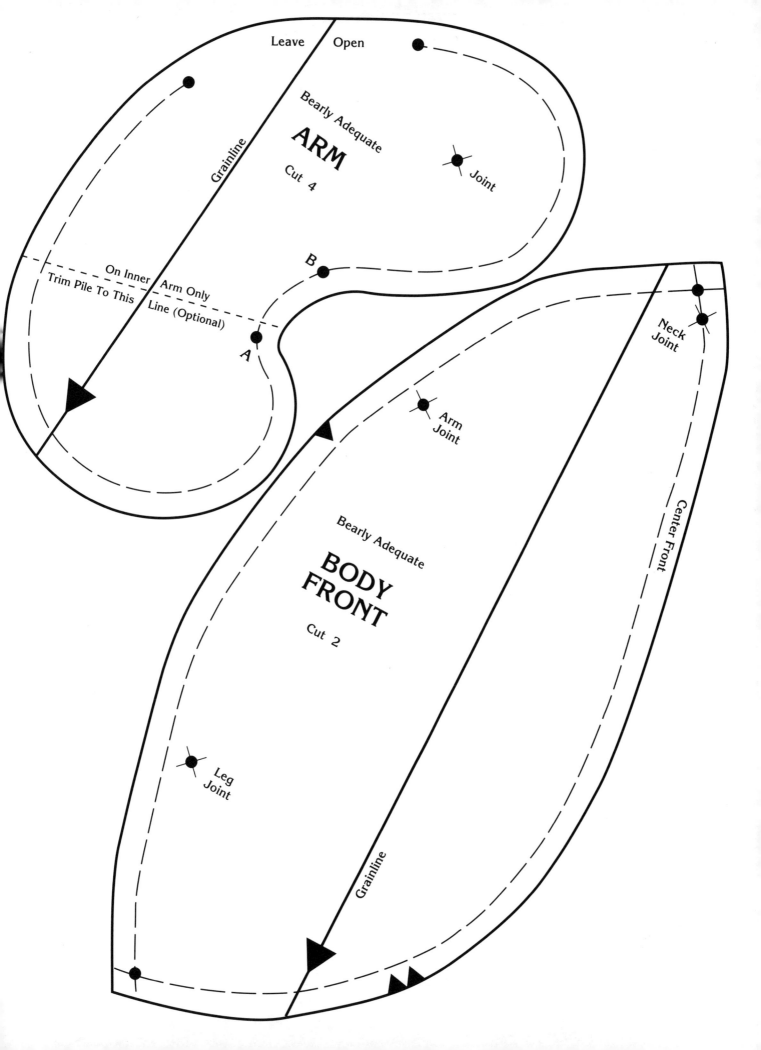

Leave   Open

Bearly Adequate

ARM

Cut 4

Grainline

Joint

B

On Inner   Arm Only

Trim Pile To This   Line (Optional)

A

Neck
Joint

Arm
Joint

Bearly Adequate

**BODY
FRONT**

Cut 2

Center Front

Leg
Joint

Grainline

8. Cubby Cousins

Jointed Bear With Cross Stitched Quilt

**Finished height: 15"
(See color pages.)**

When you hear the words "teddy bear," what image comes to mind? It's probably a generic teddy bear with body and limbs along traditional lines. Maybe your imaginary bear is fully jointed, made in a golden mohair with felt paw pads, and stuffed with excelsior.

I bet he has a wonderfully wise and patient expression...and a center gusset in his head. Such designs have been with us since the early 1900's and still grow in popularity.

This pattern is a cousin to that time-honored teddy. Cubby Cousins takes the body, arm, and leg shapes from Bearly Adequate and makes them closer to a classic jointed bear, complete with shaved paw pads and foot pads, and embroidered "claws." But that's where the similarity ends, for Cubby Cousins has a true one-piece face and a winning, soft-sculpted smile.

Fur Selection Guide:

You've already envisioned your teddy bear. Now think of the softest, smoothest, most luxurious fur you can imagine. That's how the fur pictured on the color pages feels. It is a woven German synthetic, and has the densest pile used in this book. Its sparse guard hairs extend a full 1/4" longer than the 9/16" main pile height.

Some colors of this fur are available frosted, with the top surface lighter than the base of the fibers. Frosted fur sews up beautifully because trimming the paw pads, muzzle, and inner ears adds contrast.

The Appendix lists mail-order companies that import these furs.

Materials:

1/3 yd woven fur fabric (57" wide), 9/16" pile height

Two 15mm animal eyes and their lock washers

One 24mm D-type animal nose and lock washer

Small piece of black knit suede to cover nose

One 2-3/8" growler (optional)

Nylon stocking to cover growler (optional)

Black perle cotton No. 3—thick

Polyester fiberfill

Three 45mm (1-3/4") joint sets for the head and arms

Two 55mm (2") joint sets for the legs

1 yd ribbon, 3/8" or wider

Small silk flower or holly sprig (optional)

Pattern Pieces:

Make a full set of nine pattern templates from the patterns on pages 97-101.

Cutting Directions: *Follow the fur layout diagram.*

Cut one Face. Cut two each of Body Front, Body Back, Head Back, and Foot Pad. Cut four Arms, Legs, and Ears. You should have a total of 21 fur pieces. Transfer all pattern markings to the wrongside of the fur.

Trimming the Pile:

From the rightside, holding the scissors flat against the backing, trim the pile from all 1/4" seam allowances.

Shaving the Pads:

For tips on how to shorten the pile, check Chapter 6. Shave the pile on the Foot Pads to half its original height.

Notice that the Arm pattern has a trim line. Shave the pile on the paw pads to half its original height, from the tip of the paw up to the marked line. Trim only the inner arms, one right and one left. (Do not shave the outer arms.)

Sewing Directions: *All seam allowances are 1/4".*

Although Cubby Cousin's pattern pieces are different, their construction mimics two other patterns in this book. Follow Bearly Adequate's pinning and sewing directions for the Body, Arms, Legs, and Foot Pads, beginning on page 74. To assemble the Face, Head and Ears, follow the pinning and sewing directions for the large size Chubby Cubby (beginning on page 128). Marking the pages with paper clips may help. With a pencil, circle the applicable steps from each set of directions.

Jointing and Stuffing:

After completing the machine sewing and turning the pieces to the rightside, install a 45mm joint at the neck.

Following the directions for Chubby Cubby (starting on page 131), stuff the head, sculpt the face, embroider the smile, and close the head opening.

When trimming the muzzle, follow the directions on page 133. At the end, instead of trimming only the guard hairs for the muzzle, shorten all the pile in the muzzle area about 1/8" (to a height of 7/16"). For Cubby Cousin's longer fur, this extra trimming will differentiate the muzzle from the face.

Joint the arms and legs and complete the stuffing according to Bearly Adequate's directions. See pages 79 and 80. Do not stitch the openings closed yet.

Embroidering the "Claws":

Place pins corresponding to Fig. 8.2 for the outside of the arms, and Fig. 8.3 for the legs. Remove the pins as you work.

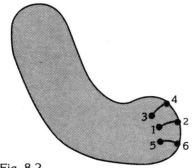
Fig. 8.2

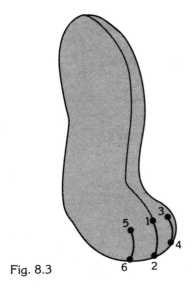
Fig. 8.3

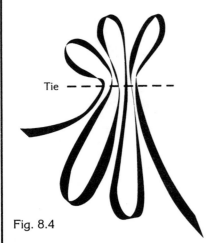
Tie
Fig. 8.4

Use a doubled length of perle cotton in a 7" soft-sculpture needle. (I use this needle because it has a large eye and extra length for gripping.) Form a knot 6" from the ends.

For both arms and legs the procedure is the same:

1. Enter your needle through the stuffing opening and bring it up at point 1.

2. Insert the needle at point 2 and bring it up at point 3. Pull the perle cotton snug, but not pinched.

3. Insert the needle at point 4 and bring it out at point 5.

4. Insert the needle at point 6, poke it all the way through the stuffing, and bring your thread out through the opening.

5. Knot your working thread to your beginning 6" tails. Clip the thread several inches from the knot and tuck the ends inside.

Finishing:

Close the openings of the arms, legs, and body with a hidden ladder stitch.

To form a depression in the ear fronts, trim the pile to half its height in the area inside the dotted line on the pattern. Finish, position, and sew the ears according to the directions for Fidget's ears, page 30.

Looped Bow:

With 1 yd of ribbon, form loops as in Fig. 8.4. Do not twist the ribbon, and make the top three loops smaller than the bottom two. Notice that the ribbon tail at the back of the bow is long, and the top end is shorter.

The easiest way to handle this bow is to have someone else

hold the loops while you tie. Second best is a clothespin or paper clip. Wrap the loops tightly with heavy-duty thread or dental tape (wide dental floss); knot with a surgeon's square knot (page 17).

If desired, tie a silk flower or a holly sprig to the bow. (Note: The bow will not be "child proof" if you add these.) With upholstery or carpet thread, securely attach the bow to the top of your teddy bear's back, near the neck joint. Knot the thread and lose the ends inside the body.

Teddy Bear's Quilt

Finished size: about 15-3/4" square
(See color pages.)

Indulge that special bear. Make him a cozy, bear-sized quilt. With it, he'll stay warm through many a cold winter's night. Select colorful fabrics for your own one-of-a-kind keepsake. After completing the cross stitch embroidery, you can finish the entire quilt by machine in just one evening.

If you've quilted before, you'll notice this quilt's 3/8" seam allowance replaces the usual 1/4". This gives you a little extra fabric in case the layers don't feed evenly into the sewing machine. My daughter started making these quilts at the age of 12. It was so much easier for her to handle the 3/8" seams, I tried it myself. I found it simplified construction, and the seam allowance made no difference in the finished quilts.

The first set of directions is for the holiday quilt with the teddy bear and candy cane. Instructions for both the Beary Merry Holly Days quilt without the stitched center block and the B-E-A-R quilt follow.

Try the charted bear design (page 96) on 22 count Hardanger, and finish as a Christmas tree ornament. Worked larger, it would make an adorable lid for a fabric-covered gift box. To use the same chart for other projects, check the table for the design area's finished measurements.

Cross Stitch Directions:

For detailed counted cross stitch directions, see Chapter 4. Also check page 82 for tips on embroidering the charted bear's face. If desired, backstitch tufts in the ears with white extra-fine hand sewing thread (as shown in color page detail).

Fig. 8.5 shows the double cross stitch for the two berries on the bear's candy cane. First do a normal cross stitch; then top it with a vertical and a horizontal stitch.

Make French Knots for the berries on the "Beary Merry Holly Days" squares. Wrap the thread twice around the needle, and, with your other hand, pull the thread to tighten the loops on the needle. Insert the needle right next to the hole you

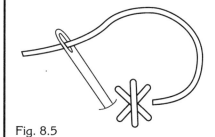

Fig. 8.5

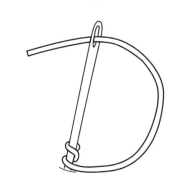

Fig. 8.6

started in (Fig. 8.6). As you pull the needle to the back of your work, hold the loops in position with your thumb.

Materials for Bear with Candy Cane Quilt:

Finished bear design worked on a 6" square of 18 count green Aida.

Finished "Beary Merry Holly Days" designs (page 97), each worked on an individual 4" square of 14 count white Aida
1/2 yd fleece or lightweight quilt batting

1/2 yd red print material (100% cotton) for backing

1/4 yd green pin-dot material (100% cotton) for binding

Remnants of coordinated, holiday print fabrics (100% cotton preferred) for quilt strips. See the cutting directions for color and pattern requirements. If possible, select several fabrics with a holly motif to tie in with the quilt's theme.

Cutting Directions:

All fabric should be cut on the straight of the grain (either lengthwise or crosswise).

Cut one 17" square of red print fabric for the backing. Cut one 17" square of quilt batting.

For the quilt strips, cut strips of fabric 2-3/4" wide. If you prefer, tear all-cotton fabrics along the crosswise grain into strips. See page 97. Strips A, B, C, and D are four different red print fabrics. I, J, K, and L are also red print fabrics. Strips E and F are green print, and strips G and H are white print.

Quilt Assembly:

1. Hand-baste the 17" square of batting to the wrongside of the 17" square of backing material.

2. Keeping the bear design centered, carefully trim the green Aida square to measure 3-3/4" by 3-3/4". Pin this square, rightside up, centered on top of the batting. Check that the raw edges of the Aida square run parallel to the raw edges of the backing material. Hand baste through all three thicknesses (Aida, batting, and backing material). See Fig. 8.7.

3. Throughout construction, maintain all the seams parallel to the backing's raw edges. Begin and end each seam 3/8" inside the raw edges. After stitching each quilt strip, trim it even with the edge of the previously sewn strips. Open that strip so the rightside is up; finger press flat. (Do not iron the quilt.)

4. For quilt strip A, place a strip of red print fabric face down on the center Aida square, raw edges even with the top of the Aida. Pin the strip, matching the upper left corner (Fig. 8.8). Place a pin 3/8" inside the Aida's right edge to mark where to stop stitching. Using a walking foot, if available, machine sew 3/8" inside the top edge of the Aida square, beginning and ending your stitching 3/8" from the side edges of the Aida. Stitch through all thicknesses (strip A, Aida, batting, and backing). Trim this strip even with the edge of the Aida. (Strip A will measure 2-3/4" by 3-3/4"). Open this strip out (Fig. 8.9).

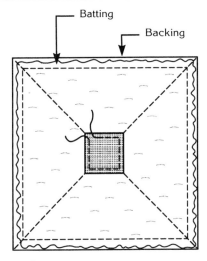

Fig. 8.7

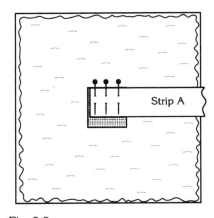

Fig. 8.8

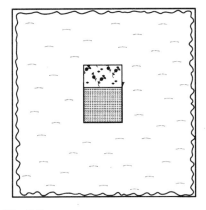

Fig. 8.9

5. Sew strip B to the bottom of the center Aida square, following the directions for strip A.

6. Carefully trim the four white Aida squares, "Beary," "Merry," "Holly," and "Days," to measure 2-3/4" by 2-3/4".

7. Before stitching, cut quilt strips C and D to each measure 2-3/4" by 3-3/4" long. With rightsides together and raw edges even, seam a short end of quilt strip C to the bottom edge of the "Beary" square. Seam the opposite end of strip C to the top edge of the "Holly" square.

8. Place this strip C, with the attached Aida squares, face down on the center of the quilt. (Fig. 8.10) Pin, matching the raw edge of strip C with the left side of the green Aida square. Make sure the "Beary" square is at the top, aligned with the short end of quilt strip A, and the "Holly" square is aligned with strip B. Check that the seams line up with the previously sewn strips. Stitch a straight 3/8" seam from the bottom of the "Holly" square, through strip C, to the top of the "Beary" square. Open flat. Repeat these steps for the right side of the quilt's center section, using strip D and the remaining "Merry" and "Days" Aida squares.

9. Following the placement on page 97, construct the quilt face by adding individual strips

in alphabetical order. Each strip is sewn according to the prior directions for strip A.

10. After completing the face of the quilt, trim the batting and backing material even with the outside edges of quilt strips I, J, K, and L.

Quilt Binding:

1. Using the green pin-dot cotton fabric, cut or tear two crosswise strips 3" wide and about 1 yd long. Fold these binding strips in half, lengthwise, wrongsides together. Iron to form a center crease along the entire length.

2. Cut one binding strip the same length as the top edge of the quilt, and one binding strip the length of the bottom edge. These should measure approximately 15-3/4" each, but the size may vary.

3. Working from the back of the quilt, pin the appropriate binding strip to the top edge, having all raw edges even. Treat the double layer of the binding as one layer. Stitch in a 3/8" seam.

4. Open out this binding, folding it over the top raw edge of the quilt. On the quilt front, pin the creased edge of the binding

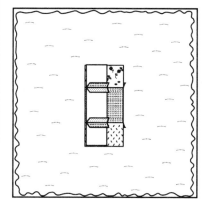

Fig. 8.10

over your stitching line. Hand-baste, if you wish. Topstitch the binding close to its crease, making sure the binding covers the previous stitching line.

5. Bind the bottom edge of the quilt, following the same directions.

6. Cut two binding strips, each 1-1/4" longer than the measurement of the unfinished sides of the quilt.

7. Pin one of these binding strips on the back of the quilt along one unbound edge. Treat the double layer of binding as one layer. The ends of the binding should extend 5/8" at the top and bottom corners. Stitch.

8. Open out the binding and turn the quilt to the rightside. Fold the 5/8" extensions to the inside at both corners, then fold the binding strip over the raw edges. Pin the creased edge of the binding over your stitching line; topstitch close to

the crease. Repeat this step for the remaining unbound edge.

9. Remove any basting threads.

Holiday Quilt with Plain Center Square:

The materials for this version are identical to the previous list, but without the green Aida center square. Instead, cut a 2-3/4" square of cotton fabric for the center block. I like to cut the center square from the same material as the binding.

All construction is the same as the previous quilt, except for the measurements. Because you start with a smaller center block, the finished quilt will be an inch smaller. Cut quilt strips A, B, C, and D to measure 2-3/4" square (rather than rectangular).

B-E-A-R Quilt:

This quilt also uses the 2-3/4" center block. Embroider the letter motifs (page 98) on individual 4" squares of 11 count white Aida. (Although the embroidery is done on Aida 11 rather than Aida 14, the finished blocks are still trimmed the same size.) If desired, change the charted floss colors to match your fabrics.

CUBBY
COUSINS
Layout
1/3 yd

Nap
Direction

↓

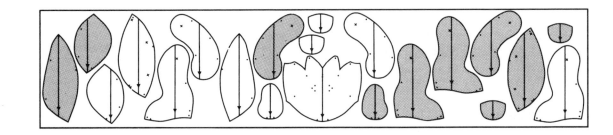

KEY   DMC COLOR NUMBER:

KEY	DMC COLOR NUMBER:
• •	3047 Yellow Beige, light
▽ ▽	3046 Yellow Beige, medium
— —	746 Off White
⌐ ⌐	822 Beige Gray, light
✕ ✕	642 Beige Gray, medium
I I	White
▲ ▲	321 Christmas Red
∩ ∩	904 Parrot Green, very dark
◇ ◇	703 Chartreuse
■ ■	666 Christmas Red, bright (double cross stitch)
	938 Nose
	3371 Eyes and Mouth
	White Eye Highlight

OUTLINE

⌐	3371 Black Brown
⋯⋯	642 Beige Gray, Medium
⧄	895 Christmas Green, dark (shadow)

Stitch Count: 43 high by 33 wide

Threads per inch of fabric	Finished design size in inches
Hardanger 22	2 by 1-1/2
Aida 18	2-3/8 by 1-7/8
Aida 14	3 by 2-3/8
Aida 11	3-7/8 by 3

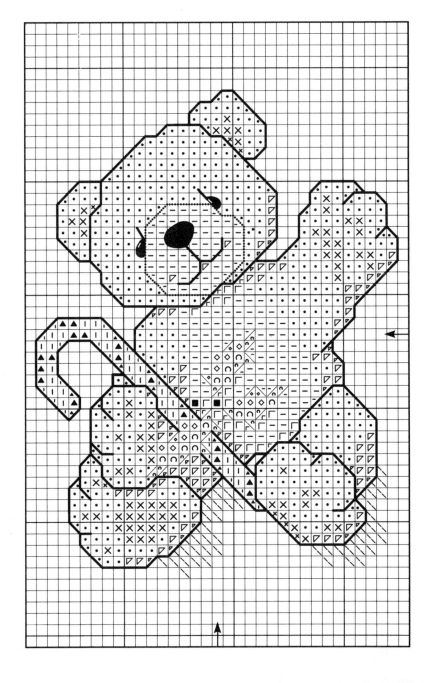

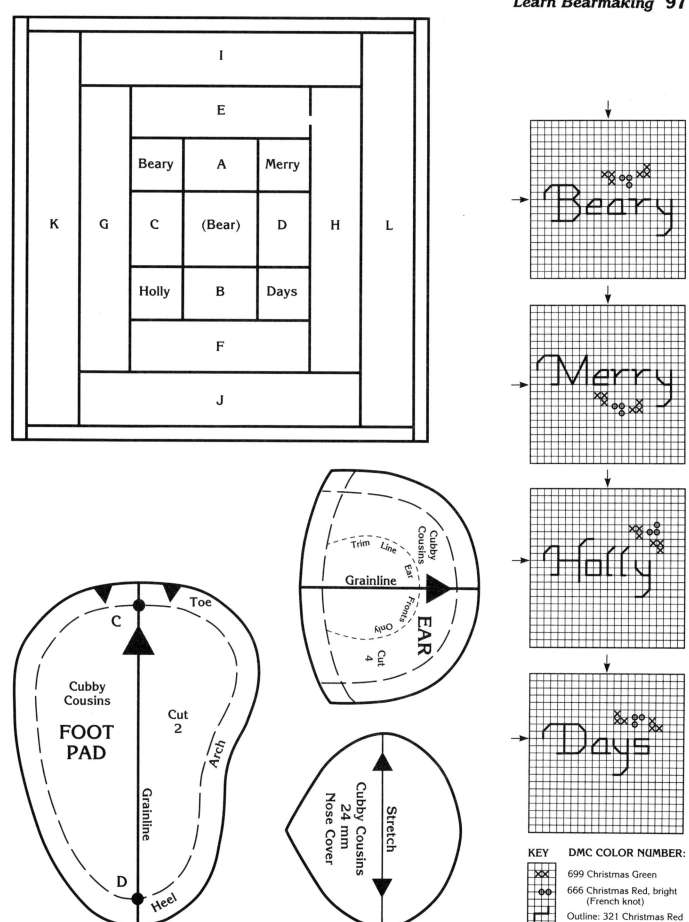

I

E

Beary | A | Merry

K | G | C | (Bear) | D | H | L

Holly | B | Days

F

J

Toe

C

Cubby
Cousins

FOOT
PAD

Cut
2

Arch

Grainline

D | Heel

Cubby
Cousins
Ear

Trim Line

Grainline

Fronts

Only

EAR

Cut
4

Cubby
Cousins
24 mm
Nose Cover

Stretch

KEY   **DMC COLOR NUMBER:**

699 Christmas Green

666 Christmas Red, bright
(French knot)

Outline: 321 Christmas Red

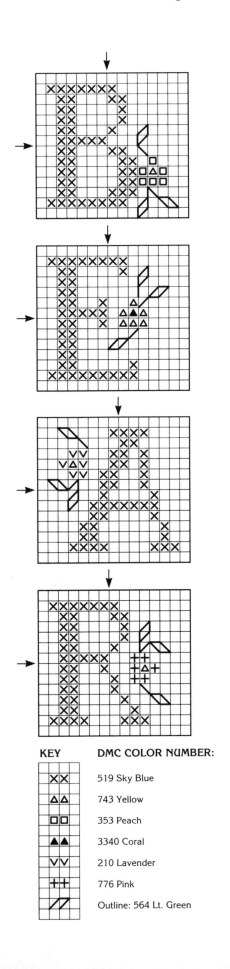

KEY   **DMC COLOR NUMBER:**

✗✗	519 Sky Blue
△△	743 Yellow
▢▢	353 Peach
▲▲	3340 Coral
✔✔	210 Lavender
✚✚	776 Pink
⧄	Outline: 564 Lt. Green

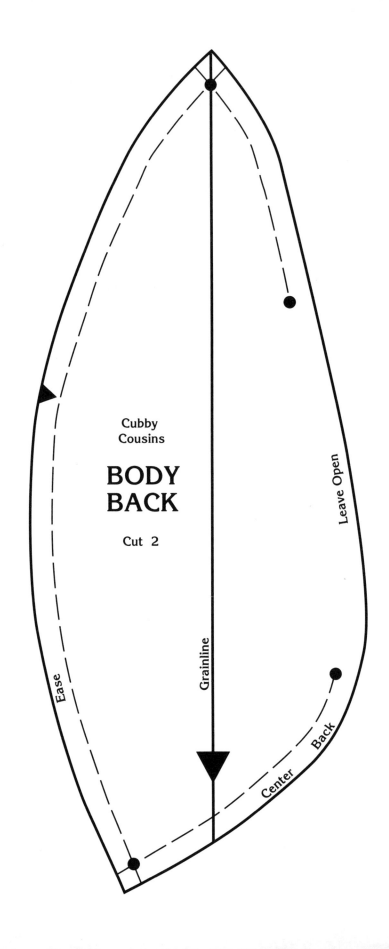

Cubby
Cousins

**BODY
BACK**

Cut 2

Grainline

Leave Open

Ease

Center Back

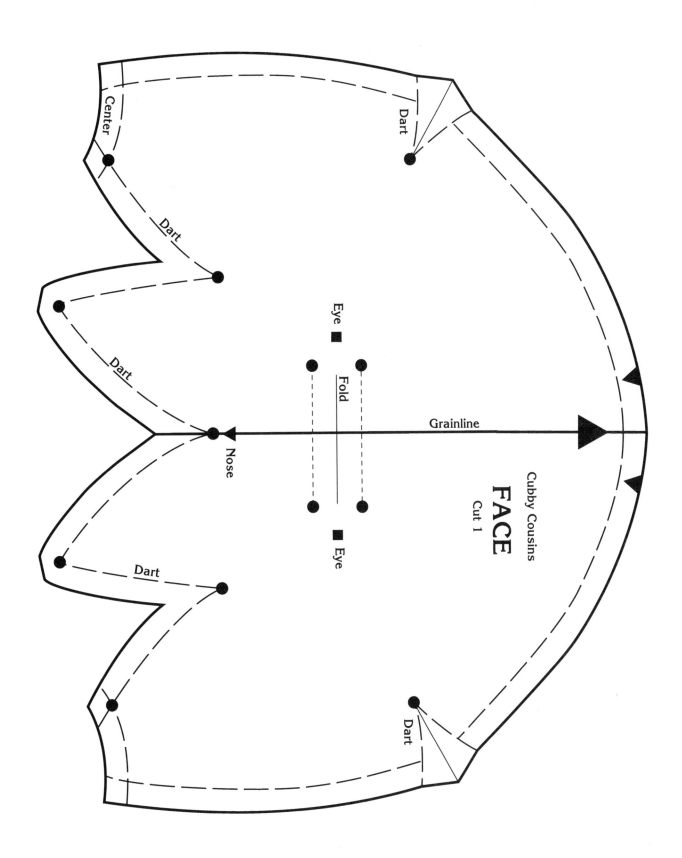

Center

Dart

Dart

Dart

Nose

Eye ■

● ●

Fold

Grainline

▶

Cubby Cousins

FACE

Cut 1

Eye ■

● ●

Dart

Dart

Dart

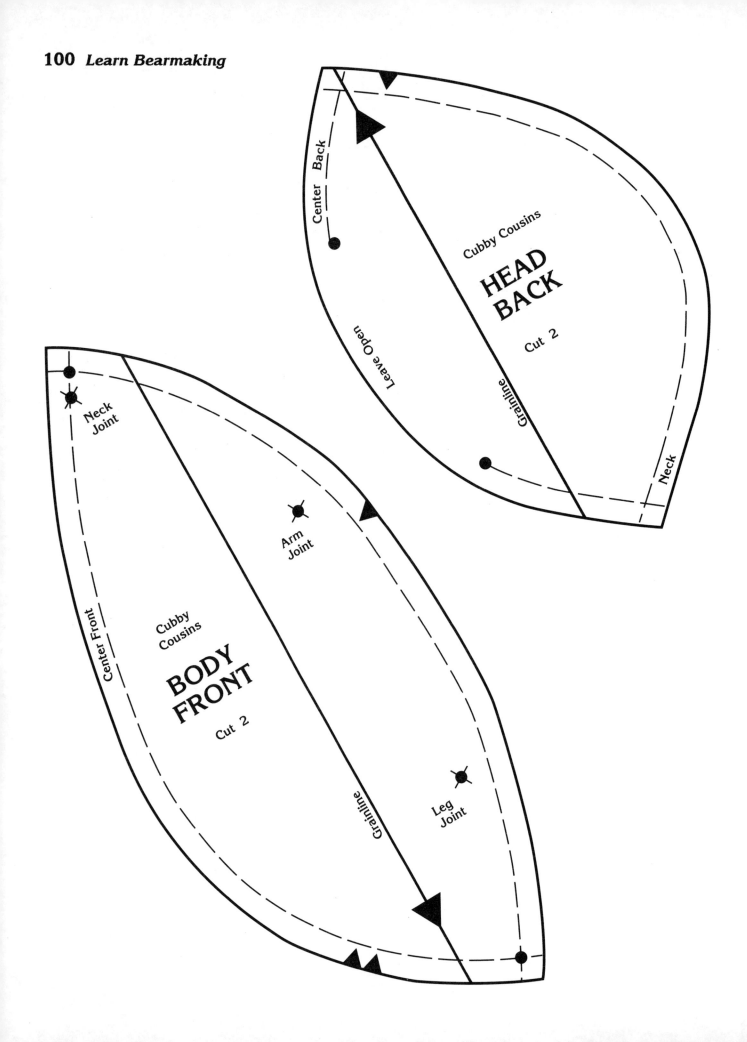

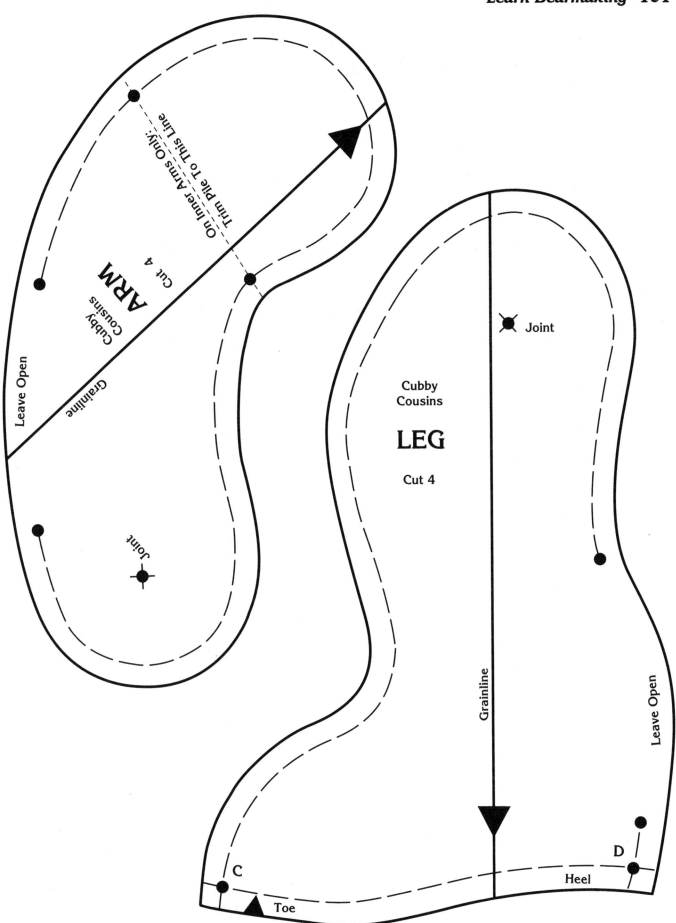

ARM
Cubby Cousins
Cut 4

On Inner Arms Only: Trim Pile To This Line

Grainline

Leave Open

Joint

LEG
Cubby Cousins
Cut 4

Joint

Grainline

Leave Open

C

Toe

Heel

D

9. Exbeartise

Advanced Techniques

You've now mastered the basic and intermediate bearmaking skills. This chapter looks at some optional tools and discusses an advanced jointing technique. It also explains how to preview your bear's expression instead of automatically installing the eyes and nose at the marked pattern locations. And finally, before you tackle Chapter 11's Chubby Cubby, read how to tint fur pile.

Tools of the Trade

Chapter 2 presented the bear necessities of bearmaking tools and supplies. Here's a sampling of other useful tools.

Leather Thimble: Also called a Pioneer Thimble™, this covers your entire finger and accomplishes two tasks. First, it cushions your index finger when pinning. Even with plastic-headed quilting pins, if you do several bears at a time, your finger will appreciate some protection. Second, you can wear it on your baby finger. When sewing by hand, do you have the habit of tugging on the thread by wrapping it against your little finger? Heavy-duty thread can bother your finger, and a leather thimble lessens this problem. See Fig. 9.2.

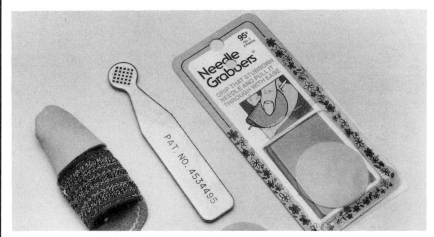

Fig. 9.1 Special tools make hand sewing easier. Left to right: leather thimble, Quilting Thimble, Needle Grabbers®.

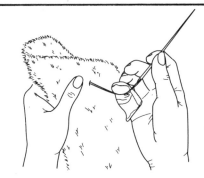

Fig. 9.2 Protect your hand with a leather thimble if you tighten the thread against your baby finger.

Fig. 9.3 A Quilting Thimble pushes the needle through firmly stuffed pieces.

Quilting Thimble: This steel paddle should be called a needle pusher instead of a thimble. You hold it rather than wear it, and use it to push the needle through stubborn areas (Fig. 9.3). It is especially helpful when working with large needles and thick perle cotton. Also, repeated yanking on hand sewing thread can tire the fingers. Try working several stitches at a time and then winding the thread around the quilting thimble's neck. Hold the wound thread in place with your thumb, and tighten by pulling on the tool, rather than on the thread itself.

Needle Grabbers®: For pulling a slippery needle through a tough spot, these rubber circles excel. And when my index finger and thumb tire, I use a needle grabber for all hand work. Other needle grippers include: rubber fingers (from office supply stores), special thimbles with grip channels, and fingers cut from surgeon's gloves.

Crock Sticks®: Early on, seamstresses learn not to cut paper with their good fabric shears. But synthetic furs and their backings dull shears faster than paper. Ever since a fabric store "sharpened" (read "ruined") my $27.00 shears, I've sharpened the blades myself. My favorite method uses Crock Sticks®, sold at cutlery shops. (See Fig. 9.4.) On some shears, like Ginghers, sharpen only the blade with the knife edge. As you sharpen blades, the crockery stick will develop a silver coating that looks like pot marks in a sink. Rotate it in its wooden base to find an uncoated area. Cleaning the sticks with kitchen cleanser restores them.

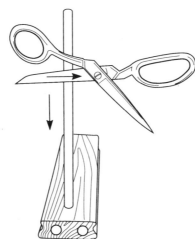

Fig. 9.4 (a) With the blade vertical and the tip pointing away from you, place the cutting edge of your shears against the crockery stick, matching the angle of the blade's ground edge. Start with the base of the blade against the top of the stick. (b) Draw the blade down the stick, pulling the handle of the shears toward you. This takes some force; pretend you are trying to "pare" the crock stick. Always keep the angle of the blade consistent. Repeat steps a and b until the blade is sharp.

Grooming Brushes: Pet shops carry two types of dog brushes, shown in Fig. 9.5. A brush with straight wire bristles set in a rubber base will do a marvelous job brushing teddy bears with 1" pile. For shorter furs, try a "slicker" brush. This rectangular brush has shorter, tightly spaced, fine, bent wire bristles that lift the nap.

Hair Dryer: Here's a way to dust your growing bear collection. You'll need a hair dryer with four settings. Set it for air only—no heat—and it will fluff your bears.

Secure Joints

Many bearmakers have used bolt and locknut joints for years, with few problems. But I also know some who have had properly installed locknuts loosen over time. When I first tried to solve this potential problem, I became frustrated with unworkable solutions, like epoxy on the threads of the bolt, or special products that were supposed to freeze the nut and bolt into one assembly—they didn't.

We teddy bear makers are not alone in our search for the perfect fastener. My dad, an engineer, told me fasteners are one of the most troublesome hardware products.

Although there is no ideal answer, the best solution I've found is a standard jam nut, available in hardware stores (Fig. 9.6). Jam nuts are thinner than regular nuts, but come in the same sizes. They add less weight to your bear than normal nuts.

Install the joint following the directions in Chapter 6. Once you have the joint tightened to

Fig. 9.5 A brush like the one on the left works well on long furs. The slicker brush on the right is better for shorter naps.

Fig. 9.6 A 1/4" jam nut (left), a regular 1/4" nut (middle), and a 1/4" locknut (right).

your satisfaction, thread a 1/4" jam nut on the same bolt, above the locknut, as in Fig. 9.7. Holding the locknut stationary with a 7/16" open-end wrench (Fig. 6-19), use a ratchet wrench or box wrench to force the jam nut down tightly against the locknut. (Note that you do not have a tool on the bolt itself in this final step.) You'll find this assembly less prone to loosening than the locknut alone.

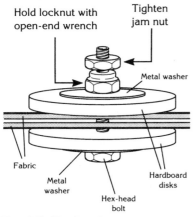

Fig. 9.7 Force a jam nut on top of the locknut to prevent loosening.

Customized Expressions

Safety eyes and noses have one drawback: they must be installed before stuffing the head. That makes previewing a bear's expression difficult...but not impossible. A little ingenuity will allow you to experiment with different placements to achieve an expression you like.

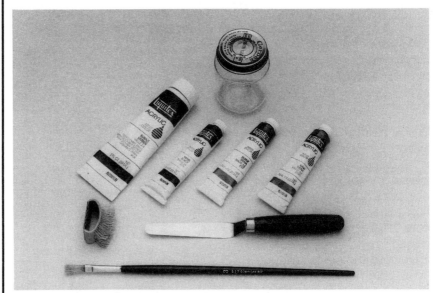

Fig. 9.8 Supplies for tinting fur pile: artist's acrylic paint, paintbrush, small jar, palette knife, and Bunka brush.

Delay the eye and nose installation until the entire bear has been stuffed. Close all the openings except the head opening with a hidden ladder stitch. You'll need some substitutes for the safety eyes and nose to help you visualize the bear's personality. Possibilities include black button eyes the right size, or a pair of glass eyes cut from their wires, or a pair of safety eyes with their shanks sawed off with a hacksaw.

An easier idea is to cut circles of black coat wool or felt the same size as the eyes, and a triangle like the nose shape, and pin these on the face. A regular dressmaker's pin simulates a highlight, and adds life to an otherwise flat, black felt. Placing eyes closer and ears higher makes a comical bear. Eyes lower and further apart, and ears to the sides rather than top of the head, gives more of an innocent, "baby" expression.

Remember that you can vary the size of the eyes and nose, as well as their location. Once you have decided on the placement, remove the stuffing from head, attach the eyes as directed in Chapter 3, and re-stuff the head.

Tinting Pile

Although some teddy bear makers tint fur fabrics with an airbrush, it is possible to achieve some lovely results without expensive equipment. The following technique works best on medium to light furs rather than dark. You'll need only a few supplies.

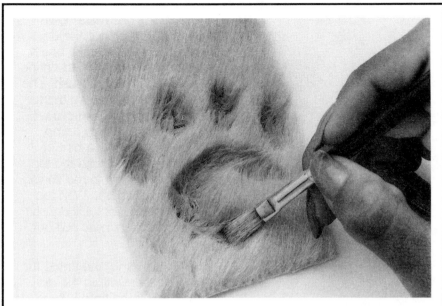

Fig. 9.9 Always do a sample test to make sure you have mixed the correct amount of paint and water. Some acrylic colors dry lighter, while others dry darker.

Artist Acrylic Paint: I use small tubes of Liquitex® acrylic colors, but any comparable brand will do. This paint thins with water and cleans up with soap and water. It is non-toxic and permanent on cloth. Once dry, the colors are supposedly machine washable (a theory you won't test with your finished teddy, anyway).

For many furs, a nice, warm brown like Burnt Umber is the only color you'll need. But any colors may be mixed. Earth tones like Burnt Sienna (adds reddish tone), Raw Sienna (tan), Yellow Ochre (gold), and Raw Umber (cooler brown) mix excellent teddy bear colors. Add Paynes Gray or Mars Black for a brown with a taupe cast. Art supply stores often display charts showing how to mix specific colors.

Artist's Paint Brush: Try a white bristle flat #3. Although this brush is flat rather than round, here the word "flat" refers to the length of the bristles (as opposed to the shorter-bristled "brights.") A #3 brush measures about 1/4" wide with bristles 11/16" long. The longer bristles hold more paint for the fabric to absorb, but the actual size is not critical. With proper care, one paint brush will last for years. Rinse it in soap and water; then dry it inverted in a jar, bristles up.

Jars: A medium one for water and a small one (like a baby food jar) for paint.

Mixing Stick: A palette knife or a popsicle stick works well.

Hair Dryer: For the preview test only.

Bunka Brush: See Fig. 9.11.

Mixing the Paint

Acrylic paints dry fast, so keep your brush wet while working. And because the diluted paint mildews in a few days, you'll probably need to mix a new batch for each bear.

1. Select the appropriate paint color(s) for your fur.

2. Put a small dab of paint in a jar. Add a couple of table-spoons of water and mix thoroughly. The solution will be thin and liquid—the more water, the lighter the color. It is better to mix the color thinner because you can always darken it with a second coat. Nothing cures a color that dries too dark.

3. Adjust the color by adding tiny amounts of other colors, if necessary. Try to mix a color a few shades darker than your fur—one that coordinates well with it. Make sure all paint has dissolved.

4. Do a preview swatch test. Before the paint touches your bear's fur, you must see how it dries. Saturate a small area on a scrap of fur fabric and let dry. To speed the drying time, use a warm hair dryer on the sample. (Never use a heated dryer on the actual bear.)

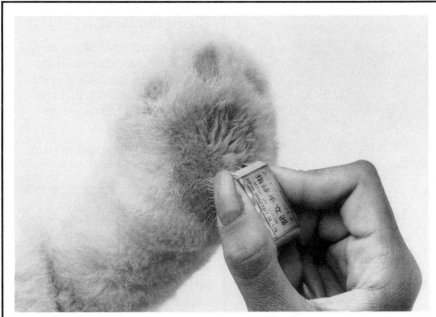

Fig. 9.10 When the pile is almost completely dry, gently brush the matted pile. With the proper paint and water solution, the tinted pile should feel as silky as the regular pile.

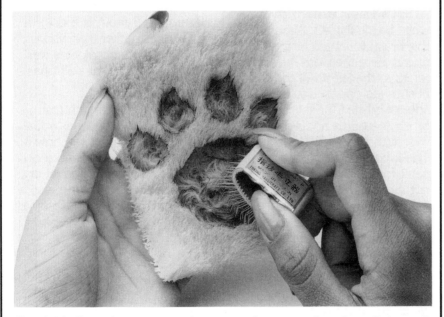

Fig. 9.11 If you have too much paint in the water, the pile will dry stiff and brittle. Either the pile will pull out in clumps when you try to brush it, or the fibers will still feel rough even after repeated brushings.

5. Since the pile mats down when wet, brush out the dry, tinted pile with a Bunka brush to restore it. The trick to tinting is knowing when to brush. The ideal time is just before the fur is completely dry. The pile will feel cool, rather than damp, and will retain only a hint of moisture. If you brush the fur too soon, when it is too moist, the paint will smear. Wait too long, and the paint will dry stiff and some fibers may pull out when brushed.

6. After brushing, the tinted fur should feel as soft as the un-treated fur. If the tinted fibers are thick, coarse, and clump together, you need to add more water to your paint. If the color dried too light, try a second coat over the first. Dry and brush it again.

Are you happy with the color? Some acrylic paints change when they dry, and you'll need to adjust your mixture to compensate. Continue to do sample tests until the dried swatch is precisely what you want. Then follow Chubby Cubby's directions for tinting the pre-shortened pile on his ears, paws, and feet. The tinted pile takes anywhere from a few hours to more than a day to air dry, depending on the temperature, humidity, and the fur's density. And tinting all the pile at once doesn't guarantee it will dry simultaneously. For instance, the fingers absorb less paint and usually dry faster.

At this point, you've covered all the techniques. Now apply what you've learned by constructing one of the advanced patterns. And for those who can't decide between Cub-bykins and Chubby Cubby, I'll offer this advice: make both.

Cubbykins. Not all bears hibernate for winter: this one enjoys the out-of-doors. Wearing his hand-knit vest and stocking cap, he builds a Snowbear. Cubbykins stands 13" tall and has jointed arms, legs, and head. (He even has eyelashes!)

Chubby Cubby. While the 14" Chubby Cubby strings a Cat's Cradle on his tinted paws, the smaller one (11") stacks holiday blocks. The Christmas theme carries through a stuffed heart pillow and holiday quilts with either a plain or an embroidered center square (see detail).

you are loved beary much

Wispy. This bubbling babe is easy to make. Her 20" non-jointed pattern has large pieces designed for a minimum of hand sewing. The perky wisps in her ears are optional. Wispy wears a ready-made infant's dress (size 6 months) and disposable diapers.

BUBBLES

Cubby Cousins. Taking a break from playing with his stuffed C-U-B blocks, this 15" teddy bear clutches his security blanket (an appealing B-E-A-R quilt). Cubby Cousins features a luxurious, woven synthetic fur, shaved paw and foot pads, and an endearing, soft-sculpted smile.

Bearly Adequate. These sweethearts are made in a cuddly, 1"-pile fur. One 17" bear offers his heart, while the other returns the requested hug. Both bears will steal your heart when you add your own hugs.

I want a hug

Cubbykins. Crescent-shaped fingers and toes and a contrasting tummy set 13" Cubbykins apart from other teddies. Those nimble fingers knit up a variegated vest and cap in the blink of an eyelash. Check the knitting instructions, and you can join this act, too.

Fidget. You'll find this 10" puppet is aptly named. Insert your hand and Fidget comes to life with his personality--and some of your own. Although his lining hides a squeaker, he sometimes snuggles in a splendid, personalized Christmas stocking, hardly making a sound.

(left) ***Chubby Cubby.*** Good things come in small packages. This Chubby Cubby might be one of the smallest bears in this book, but he doesn't have one fraction less personality. Notice the tiny reproduction of Bearly Adequate.

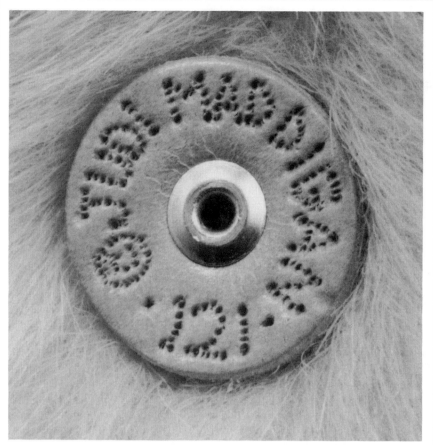

Consider marking your bears for future identification. I number my artist bears, and each (after number 100) has a 3/4" tooled leather circle riveted to his upper back. But a simple tag, like your name and the date embroidered on a ribbon that's stitched into a seam, would serve the same purpose.

In addition to a label, you might want to write a card or letter to accompany your bear. A new owner (whether a relative or not) would appreciate knowing about the bear's birth and history.

10. Cubbykins

Jointed Bear With Knit Vest and Cap

**Finished height: 13"
(See color pages.)**

What sets Cubbykins apart from other teddy bears? Is it his contrasting tummy? His two-tone ears? His crescent-shaped fingers and toes? His eyelashes?

The answer, I think, is the same quality that sets many hand-made bears apart from manufactured bears: expression. When you look into the eyes of a handmade teddy bear, you see the caring and joy placed there directly by the hands of his creator. True to his art form, Cubbykins has an expression that speaks for itself.

If you want to make your own Cubbykins, and see what his expression will say to you, don't be put off by the pattern's "advanced" label. He's not that difficult to make...he just has more pieces.

Fur Selection Guide:

This pattern, like Chubby Cubby and Cubby Cousins, uses splendid woven synthetics. Coordinate the main pile with a shorter, lighter-colored pile.

Notice a choice of pile heights for both the main and the contrast furs. Ordinarily, I like bare bears—i.e., undressed—but in Cubbykin's case, I'll make an exception: the longer pile looks chic all by itself, while a classy knit vest and stocking cap flatter a shorter nap.

The ideal eyelash fur, a dense, variegated chocolate brown, is of the same variety as Chapter 7's Bearly Adequate.

Materials:

1/4 yd woven fur fabric (57" wide) in the main color, 7/16" or 8/16" pile height

1/4 yd woven fur fabric in the contrasting color, with a pile height about 1/16" shorter than the main fur

Small piece of dark brown or black, woven or knit fur fabric with a pile height about 1" (for eyelashes—optional)

Small crochet hook—size 12 (for eyelashes)

Two 12mm animal eyes and their lock washers

One 21mm "D"-type animal nose and lock washer

Five 1-1/2" joint sets

Small piece of black knit suede to cover nose. (A dark brown, closely woven wool may be substituted.)

Black or dark brown perle cotton No. 3—thick. (Match the color of the nose material.)

One 1-7/8" growler (optional)

Nylon stocking to cover growler (optional)

Polyester fiberfill

Pattern Pieces:

Make a full set of pattern templates from the patterns on pages 121-125. You should have a total of 17 pieces.

Cutting Directions: *Follow both layout diagrams, one for main fur and one for contrast fur.*

Main Fur: Cut two each of Ear Backs, Inner Arms, Outer Arms, Leg Fronts, Leg Backs, Head Backs, and Soles. Cut one each of Face, Body Back, Body Right Side, and Body Left Side.

Contrasting Fur: Cut one Muzzle and one Body Front. Cut two each of Inner Ears, Fingers, and Toes.

You should have 26 fur pieces (18 in the main color and eight contrasting). On the wrongside, transfer all pattern markings.

Trimming the Pile:

From the rightside, holding scissors flat against the backing, trim the pile from all seam allowances. If your fur ravels, finish the opening edges. (See page 63.)

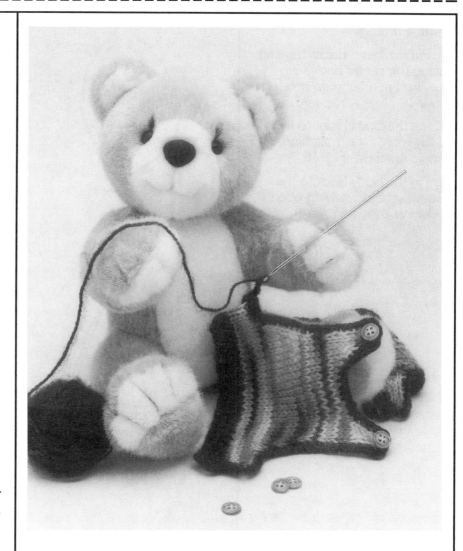

First Pinning:

1. Pin the Head Backs together along the center back seam, leaving open between dots. (Fig. 10.2)

2. Pin the Body Front to the Body Right Side, matching single notches. (Fig. 10.3)

3. Pin the Body Back to the Body Left Side, leaving open between dots. (Fig. 10.4)

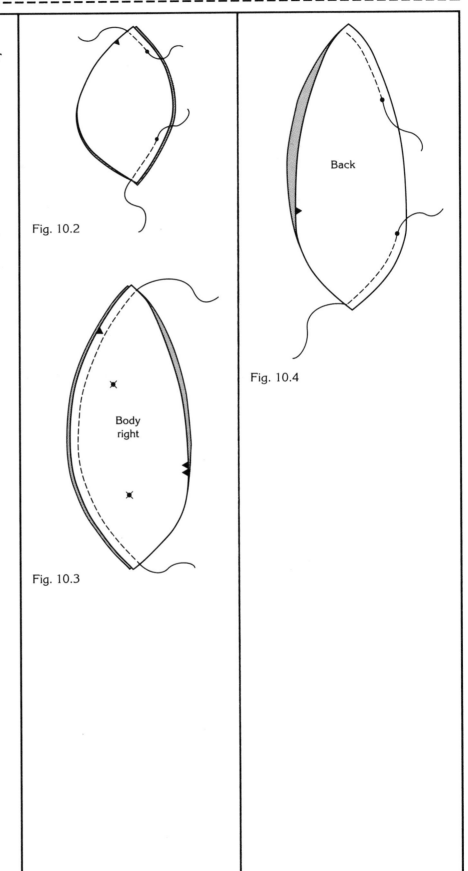

Fig. 10.2

Body right

Fig. 10.3

Back

Fig. 10.4

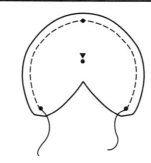

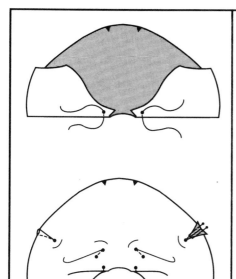

Fig. 10.5

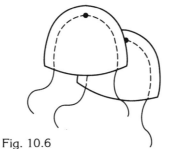

Fig. 10.6

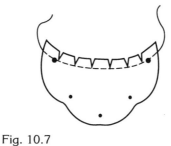

Fig. 10.7

First Stitching: *All seam allowances are 1/4".*

1. Stitch the center back seam of the head, leaving open between the dots. (Fig. 10.2)

2. Seam the Body Front to the Body Right Side. (Fig. 10.3)

3. Seam the Body Back to the Body Left Side, leaving open between dots. (Fig. 10.4)

4. Make two tucks in the Face by folding along the solid lines and stitching from the fold to the dots. Finger press the tucks down and baste in place. (Fig. 10.5)

5. Make two darts above the eyes.

6. Make two darts at the top of the Face. Slit these two darts and pin open.

7. Run a gathering stitch along the outer edge of the Muzzle and around the curved edges of the Ear Backs. Keep your stitching slightly inside the 1/4" seam allowance. (Note: The Ear Backs resemble the Soles, so make sure you have the right pieces.) (Fig. 10.6)

8. Stay stitch the fingers and the toes along their notched edges, slightly inside the 1/4" seam allowance. Clip the seam allowances to the stay stitching. (Fig. 10.7)

Second Pinning:

1. Pin the two halves of the body together, around the entire seam, matching double notches. Align the seams at the top and bottom. (Fig. 10.8)

2. Pin the Muzzle to the Face, matching centers. Below the eyes only, pull up the gathers to ease the Muzzle. (Do not gather the Muzzle between the eyes.) (Fig. 10.9)

3. Pin the Fingers to the Inner Arms, matching notches and dots. (Fig. 10.10)

4. Pin the Toes to the Soles, matching double notches and dots. (Fig. 10.11)

5. Pin the Ear Backs to the Inner Ears along the curved edges, matching dots, drawing up gathers to fit. (Fig. 10.12)

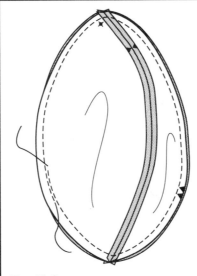

Fig. 10.8

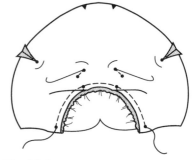

Fig. 10.9

Third Pinning:

1. Pin the center front Face seam from the nose to the neck edge, matching the Muzzle seams. (Fig. 10.13)

2. Pin an Inner Arm with the attached Fingers to the appropriate Outer Arm, leaving open between dots. Repeat for the other arm. (Fig. 10.14)

3. Pin the Soles to the Leg Backs at the heels, from point "A" to point "B," easing the Soles to fit. (Fig. 10.15)

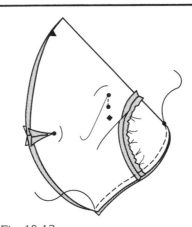

Fig. 10.13

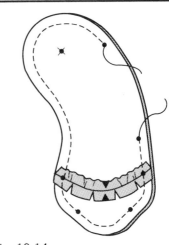

Fig. 10.14

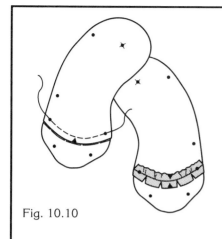

Fig. 10.10

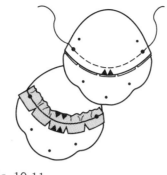

Fig. 10.11

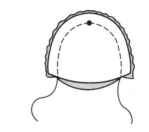

Fig. 10.12

Second Stitching:

1. Sew the body pieces together in one continuous seam. (Fig. 10.8)

2. Stitch the Muzzle seam from dot to dot, with the Muzzle toward the feed dogs. (Fig. 10.9)

3. Seam the Fingers to the Inner Arms from dot to dot. (Fig. 10.10)

4. Seam the Toes to the Soles from dot to dot. (Fig. 10.11)

5. Stitch the ears together, keeping the Ear Backs toward the feed dogs. Leave bottoms open. (Fig. 10.12)

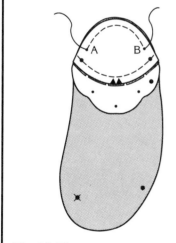

Fig. 10.15

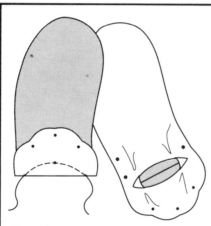

Fig. 10.16

Third Stitching:

1. Sew the center front Face seam, following the curve of the Muzzle. (Fig. 10.13)

2. Sew the arm seams, leaving open between dots for turning. (Fig. 10.14)

3. Seam the Soles to the Leg Backs, with the Soles toward the feed dogs. Begin stitching at point "A" and end at point "B." Note that you do not seam the extra 1/4" at the beginning and end of this seam. Pin the seam allowance open. (Fig. 10.15)

4. Make a dart in each Leg Front, rolling the fur between your fingers so that the stitching does not trap the pile. Trim the dart to a 1/4" seam allowance. From the wrongside, pull out any loose fur trapped in the stitching. (Fig. 10.16)

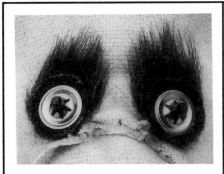

Fig. 10.17 Using an awl, poke a hole in the center of an eyelash fur circle. Push the eyelash fur onto the shaft of the eye, with the rightside of the eyelash fur against the wrongside of the face. Note that the nap of the eyelash fur goes up and points toward the top center forehead.

Fig. 10.18 Insert a small crochet hook right next to the eye, at the base of the dart. Pull fibers of the longer, dark fur through to the front for the eyelashes. Continue to pull a few hairs at a time through, until you are satisfied with the effect. Then install the locking washer on the eye in the normal way. If desired, the eyelashes can be trimmed or shortened later.

Eyes and Nose:

Note: Eyelashes are optional. Using the Eyelash pattern, cut two circles of the dark, 1" pile fur. Poke a hole with an awl for each eye where indicated on the Face, and insert the eye shanks. Before attaching the lock washers, pull eyelashes through as shown in Figs. 10.17 and 10.18.

Cover the nose and install it at the mark on the Muzzle.

Fourth Pinning:

1. Pin the Face to the Head Backs around the entire seam, matching seams and notches. (Fig. 10.19)

2. Pin a Leg Front to the appropriate Leg Back, matching points "A" and "B," leaving open where indicated. The seam allowances at points "A" and "B" should already be pinned open. Note that the Leg Front dart lines up with the Toe/Sole seam. Repeat for the other leg. (Fig. 10.20)

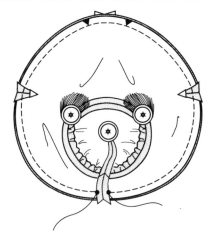

Fig. 10.19

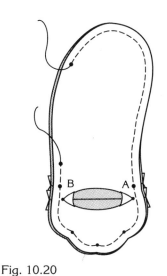

Fig. 10.20

Fourth Stitching:

1. Seam the Face to the Head Backs. Begin your stitching 1/8" to the side of the center bottom seams of the head, and end it 1/8" before you reach the center bottom again. This leaves a 1/4" gap in the stitching for the neck joint. (Fig. 10.19)

2. Seam the legs with the Leg Backs toward the feed dogs. Leave an opening in each for turning. To reinforce the ankles, stitch again over your first stitching at points "A" and "B." (Fig. 10.20)

Turning the Pieces:

Turn all fur pieces to the rightside. Check the seams for pile caught by the stitching. Free any trapped pile using the tip of a large needle.

Jointing the Head:

Install the neck joint according to the directions starting on page 68.

Stuffing the Head:

Following the directions on page 131, stuff Cubbykins's head like Chubby Cubby's (Chapter 11). The difference is that Cubbykins has a separate muzzle piece, making it easier to shape a handsome profile without forcing as much fiberfill into the muzzle area. The overall shape of the head and the firmness of the mouth area are the same for both bears.

Sculpting the Face:

Mark the location of the mouth by placing pins corresponding to Fig. 10.21. Sculpt the Face following the directions for Chubby Cubby (page 132), steps 2 through 9. Also, embroider the mouth with perle cotton. (See page 133, steps 1 through 5.)

Close the back head opening with a hidden ladder stitch.

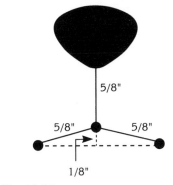

Fig. 10.21

Trimming the Expression:

Because the pile height of the muzzle is less than the face, it is not trimmed as much as Chubby Cubby's muzzle (Chapter 11). However, do clip the pile at the corners of the smile. Shorten the pile along the mouth lines and at the center front seam, between the nose and mouth, so that the perle cotton shows. Clip off any guard hairs on the upper lip, between the nose and the mouth line, and round out the shapes.

Trim any hairs that hide the eyes. Strive for teardrop-shaped eyes as in Fig.10.22. If the eyelashes overpower the expression, carefully thin or shorten them. Their effect should be subtle.

Stuffing the Arms and Legs:

Joint and stuff the arms and legs as for Chubby Cubby, page 133, but do not close the openings yet.

Fig. 10.22

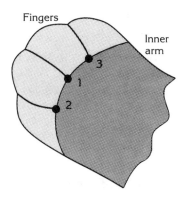

Fig. 10.23

Finger and Toe Sculpting:

Place pins corresponding to Fig. 10.23 for each arm and leg. Use a single length of perle cotton in a 7" soft-sculpture needle. Form a knot 6" from the ends.

For both arms and legs:

1. Enter your needle through the stuffing opening and bring it up at point 1.

2. Insert your needle on the opposite side of the arm or leg, directly behind point 1. Bring your thread straight up through the hand or foot to point 1. This makes a loop between the center two fingers or toes (Fig. 10.24). Tighten this loop.

3. For reinforcement, make another loop by inserting your needle directly behind point 1 again. This time, bring the needle up at point 2. Tighten the thread. (Fig. 10.25)

4. Similar to the two loops between the middle two fingers, make two loops of perle cotton at point 2, and two loops at point 3, tightening after each stitch. End by bringing your thread out through the stuffing opening.

5. Knot your working thread to the beginning 6" tail. Clip the thread several inches from the knot and tuck the ends inside.

Finishing:

Stuff the body according to the directions for Chubby Cubby.

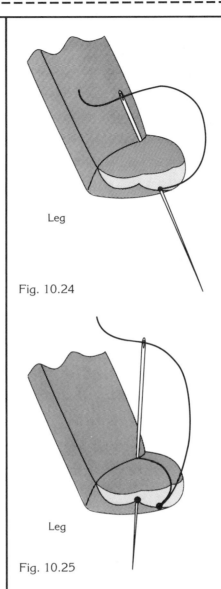

Leg

Fig. 10.24

Leg

Fig. 10.25

(See "Finish Stuffing" on page 134.)

Close all openings with a hidden ladder stitch.

Attaching the Ears:

Note that the Ear Back is larger than the Inner Ear. When you flatten the ear out, the fold line is in the Ear Back piece. This is the only pattern in this book where the ear's seams are not at the edges of the ear.

Close the bottom of the ears with a hidden ladder stitch, turning the raw edges to the inside. Pull the threads to gather the bottom slightly, shaping the ear around your thumb to form a hollow. Knot.

Position and sew the ears according to Fidget's directions, steps 2 and 3 on page 30.

Knit Vest and Cap

Hand knitting a garment usually means weeks of time. That's what's fun about knitting for teddy bears. You can finish this vest and stocking cap in less time than it takes to knit one sleeve of an adult-sized sweater.

The vest front and back (two separate pieces) button at the shoulders and sides. This permits adjustment for a perfect fit on Cubbykins. The pattern might also fit other teddy bears in your collection if they have a waist measurement of approximately 13-1/2".

Materials and Supplies:

For the variegated vest and cap (shown on the second color page), worsted weight yarn or acrylic "Fluff II" (or other yarn that will knit the same gauge): 2 oz. main color, 1 oz. contrasting color.

For the patterned vest and cap (shown on the first color page), 4-ply, worsted weight yarn: 1-1/2 oz. White; 1 oz. Kelly Green; small amounts of Chartreuse, Pink, and Cranberry.

Six 1/2" buttons

Knitting needles No. 5 and No. 7, or sizes needed for correct gauge

Small stitch holder

Crochet Hook size 00

Tapestry needle (approximately size 14)

Tape measure

3" piece of cardboard

Abbreviations:

K - knit

P - purl

st - stitch

sts - stitches

beg - beginning

tog - together

sl - slip

PSSO - pass the slipped stitch over the knit stitch

rem - remaining

sc - single crochet

ch - chain

MC - main color yarn

CC - contrasting color yarn

work even - work the established pattern without increasing or decreasing

* - repeat the directions between a pair of asterisks the given number of times.

stock st - stockinette stitch - *knit 1 row, purl 1 row*

ribbing - *knit 1 stitch, purl 1 stitch* across entire row

Gauge:

Check your gauge by knitting a sample swatch before starting your bear's garments. Change to larger or smaller needles as necessary to obtain the proper gauge.

Stockinette stitch on No. 7 needles:

5 stitches = 1"

6 rows = 1"

Knitted Vest:

These directions are for the variegated vest. Charts for the patterned vest follow the cap directions.

The directions are written for the vest front. Changes for the vest back are in parenthesis. For example, if the direction says, "cast on 33 (39) sts," when making the front, cast on 33 stitches. When you knit the back, follow the same set of directions, but cast on 39 stitches.

Front (Back):

With the smaller needles and CC, cast on 33 (39) sts loosely. Work 3 rows of ribbing (*K 1 st, P 1 st*). Break off CC, leaving a 3" tail. Change to MC and larger needles; work stock st for 5 rows. Bind off 4 sts at the beg of next 2 rows—25 (31) sts. *P 1 row. K 1, sl 1, K 1, PSSO, K to within 3 sts of end, K 2 tog, K 1* 4 (6) times—17 (19) sts. Work even for 5 (3) rows, ending with a P row.

Neck: K 6 sts; place on holder for first shoulder. Bind off 5 (7) sts. K to end. Row 1: P 6 sts. *Row 2: K 1, sl 1, K 1, PSSO, K to end. Row 3: P.* Repeat these 2 rows. (On Back only, after repeat, K 1 extra row and P 1 extra row.) Bind off rem 4 sts.

Pick up 6 sts from holder. Join MC at neck edge and work to correspond to right shoulder: Row 1: P 6 sts. *Row 2: K to within 3 sts of end, K 2 tog, K 1. Row 3: P.* Repeat these 2 rows. (Work extra rows on back.) Bind off rem 4 sts.

Crocheted Edging on Front:

With the rightside of the front facing you, join CC at lower right-hand corner with size 00 hook. Crochet up the side as follows: work 1 sc in the corner st. For the buttonholes, ch 3, skip 1 st, 1 sc in each of next 5 sts, ch 3, skip 1 st, 3 sc in corner st. Work around the armhole, shoulder, and neck edges, making 1 sc in each st and 3 sc in each corner. On the last side, after 3 sc in the lower corner of the armhole, ch 3, skip next st, 1 sc in each of next 4 sts, ch 3, skip 1 st, 1 sc in the bottom corner. End off.

Crocheted Edging on Back:

Begin at lower right corner, with rightside up. With CC, make 1 sc in each st up the side, 3 sc in corner st, and 1 sc along armhole to shoulder. For the buttonhole: 3 sc in top armhole corner, ch 3, 3 sc in top corner of neckline. Sc around neck edge. 3 sc in neckline corner, ch 3, 3 sc in armhole corner. Sc along armhole, 3 sc in lower armhole corner st, sc to lower edge and end off.

Finishing:

Weave in all yarn ends on the wrongside. Block to finished measurements on the charts. Note: Do not block ribbing.

Pin the vest front and vest back to your finished teddy bear. Note the amount of overlap you need for a good fit. Sew two buttons on each side of the back under the buttonholes; sew one button at each shoulder of the front.

Stocking Cap:

With the smaller needles and CC, cast on 58 sts loosely. Work 3 rows of ribbing (*K 1 st, P 1 st*). Break off CC, leaving a 3" tail. Change to MC and larger needles; work stock st for 5 rows, ending with a K row. Row 6: P 29, place marker, P to end. *Next row: K 1, sl 1, K 1, PSSO, K to within 3 sts of marker, K 2 tog, K 1, sl marker, K 1, K 2 tog, K to within 3 sts of end, K 2 tog, K 1. P 1 row; K 1 row; P 1 row.* Repeat these 4 rows until 10 sts remain on needle. P 1 row; K 1 row; P 1 row. K 1, *K 2 tog, K 1* 3 times. P 1 row. Slip these 7 sts on holder.

Finishing:

Weave in yarn ends. Block. The finished ribbing is 11-1/2" wide (note that this is at an angle, not straight across the bottom). The hat is 9-1/2" long.

Make a tassel: With the size 00 hook, make an 8" chain in CC; end off. Wrap CC yarn 20 times around a 3" piece of cardboard. Tie one side with the 8" chain, forming a square knot in the center of the chain. (This leaves two chain ends, each 4" long.) Cut the opposite end of the tassel and remove the cardboard. Wrap yarn around the tassel 1/2" from the knotted chain; tie. Trim the tassel to measure 2-1/4". Knot the free ends of the chain 1-1/4" away from the tassel.

Sew seam in cap: Run your tapestry needle and yarn through the 7 sts on the holder. Gather these sts around the knot in the tassel chain, having the tassel against the rightside of the knitting, sandwiched inside the point of the cap. Knot your yarn and take a couple of stitches through the chain to reinforce. With rightsides together, backstitch the side seam of the hat, being careful not to catch the tassel in the stitching. Turn to rightside.

Patterned Vest and Cap:

The five-color vest and cap are shaped in the same manner as the previous directions. Work your stockinette stitch in different colors, following the charts. When changing colors, always pick up the new color from under the previous working yarn. Don't knot new colors, but leave a 4" tail. After knitting the entire piece, adjust the tension of each color's beginning and ending stitches so that all rows are even. Then weave in the ends on the wrongside and clip off any excess yarn.

STOCKING CAP

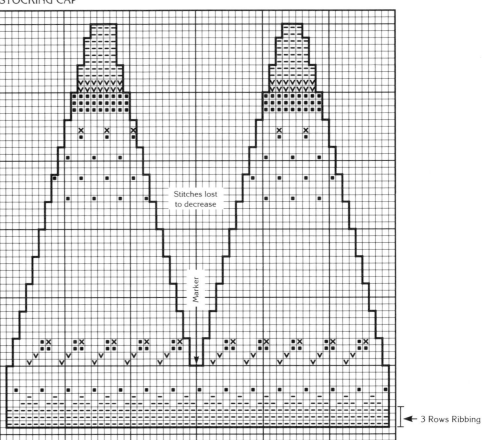

Stitches lost to decrease

Marker

← 3 Rows Ribbing

KEY

−−	Dark Green
■■	Pink
✗✗	Cranberry
✔✔	Light Green
	White

VEST BACK

5 1/2"

7 3/4"

3 Rows
Ribbing

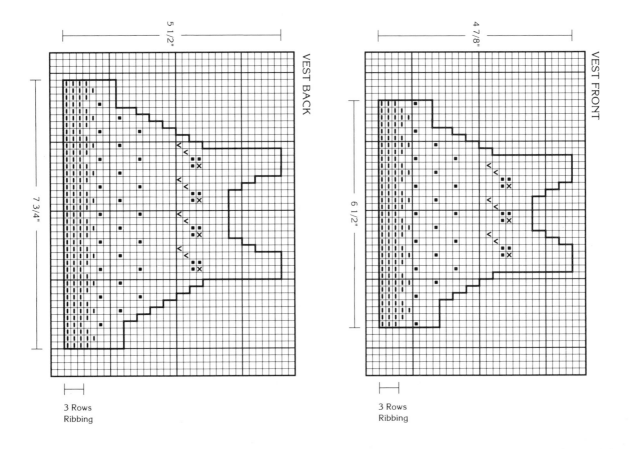

VEST FRONT

4 7/8"

6 1/2"

3 Rows
Ribbing

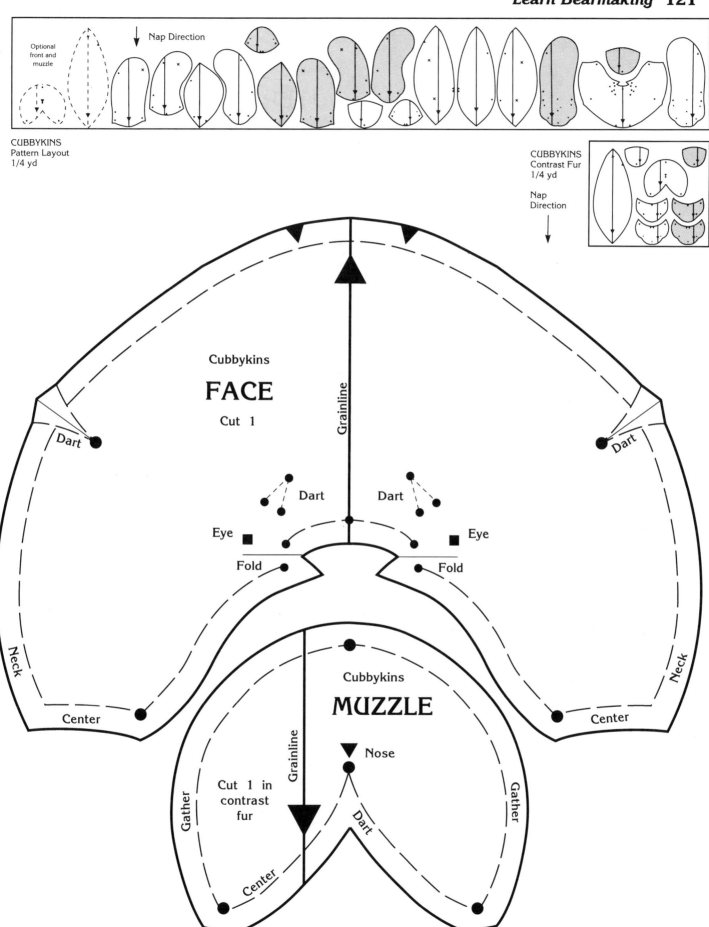

Optional
front and
muzzle

↓ Nap Direction

CUBBYKINS
Pattern Layout
1/4 yd

CUBBYKINS
Contrast Fur
1/4 yd

Nap
Direction

Cubbykins

FACE

Cut 1

Grainline

Dart

Dart

Dart

Dart

Eye

Eye

Fold

Fold

Neck

Neck

Center

Center

Cubbykins

MUZZLE

Nose

Grainline

Cut 1 in
contrast
fur

Gather

Gather

Dart

Center

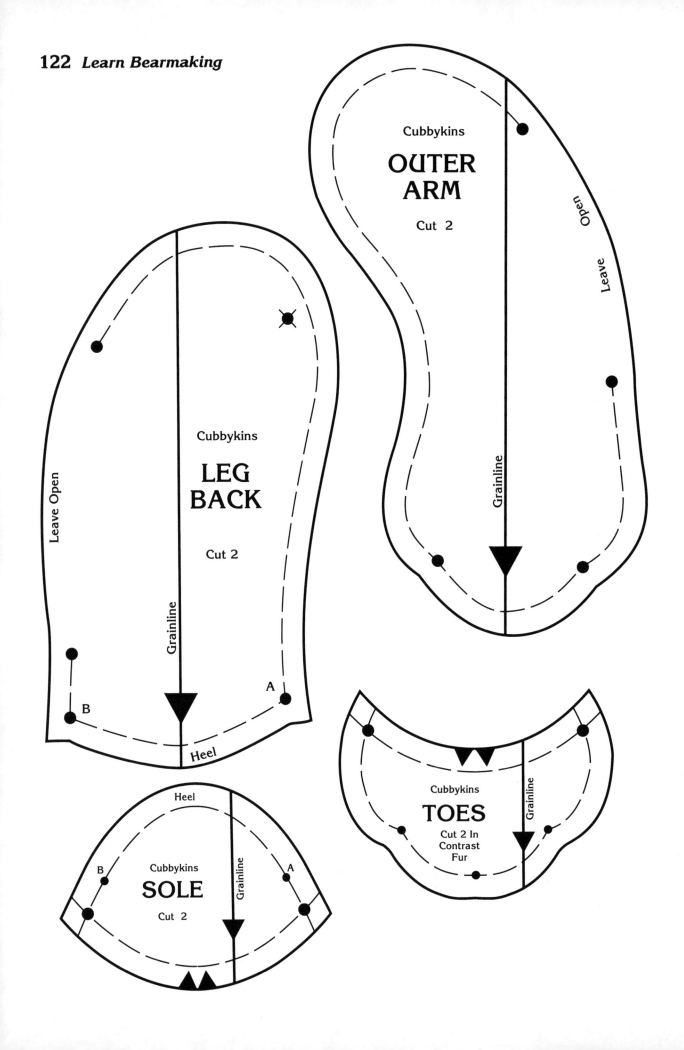

Cubbykins

OUTER ARM

Cut 2

Leave Open

Grainline

Cubbykins

LEG BACK

Cut 2

Leave Open

Grainline

A

B

Heel

Cubbykins

TOES

Cut 2 In Contrast Fur

Grainline

Heel

B

Cubbykins

SOLE

Cut 2

A

Grainline

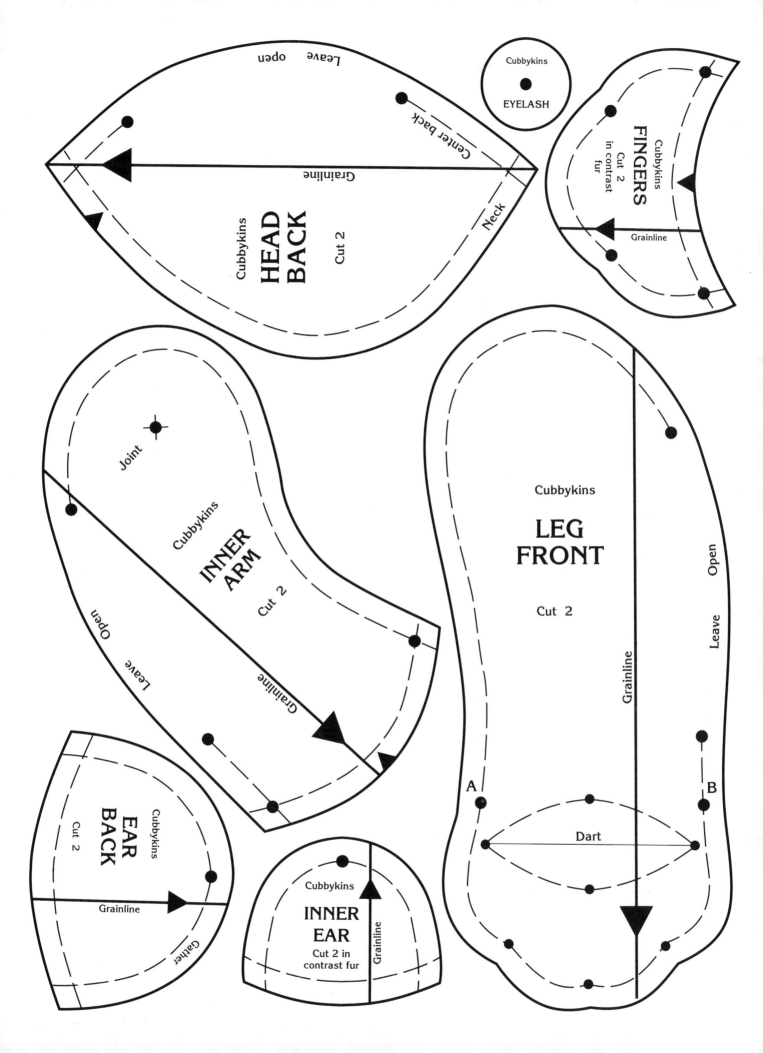

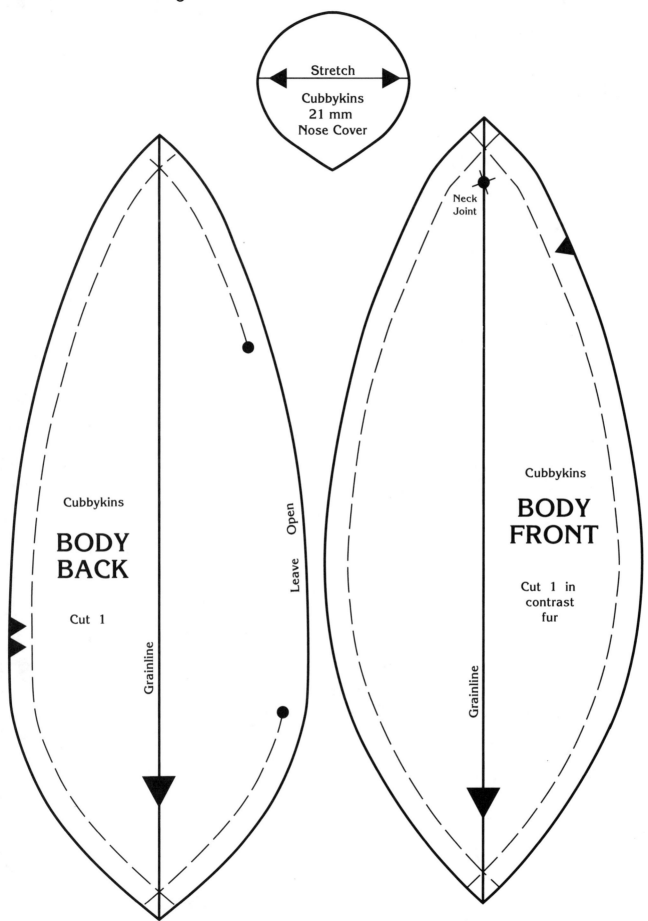

Stretch

Cubbykins
21 mm
Nose Cover

Cubbykins

**BODY
BACK**

Cut 1

Grainline

Leave   Open

Cubbykins

**BODY
FRONT**

Cut 1 in
contrast
fur

Neck
Joint

Grainline

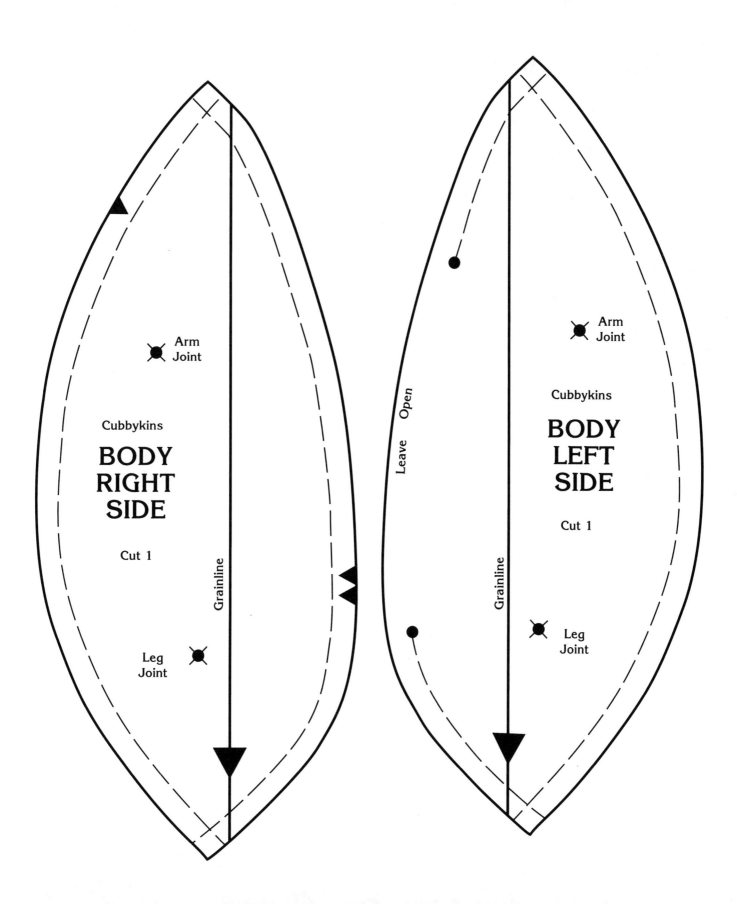

11. Chubby Cubby

Jointed Bear With Tinted Pads

Two sizes: 11" or 14" (See color pages.)

When you're a chubby cub, there's more of you to love. This little guy certainly qualifies—from the tip of his pug nose to the ends of his soft-sculpted toes.

While Chapter 8's Cubby Cousins was based on the traditional teddy shape, Chubby Cubby breaks all the rules. His roly-poly body has A-line seams, rather than center front and center back. The legs have side seams (not front and back) and incorporate the foot pads with the leg back. But Cubby's most unusual feature is the tinted paw detailing.

I also designed him in two sizes. When you make them both up, they almost look like two different bears.

Fur Selection Guide:

Chubby Cubby's pattern was designed for top quality, imported synthetic furs with 100% cotton, woven backings. A pile height slightly under 1/2" serves for both the large and the small size. Some colors are variegated; others are not.

These furs are soft and dense, with a guard hair that stands about 1/8" longer than the 7/16" main pile. This guard hair imparts a warm, fuzzy feeling to the bear. Check the Appendix for mail-order suppliers who offer sample swatch sets of their woven synthetic furs.

Materials:

For the small Chubby Cubby:

1/4 yd woven fur fabric (57" wide), 7/16" pile height

One 21mm "D"-type animal nose and lock washer

Five 1-1/2" joint sets

One 1-7/8" growler (optional)

For the large Chubby Cubby:

1/3 yd woven fur fabric (57" wide), 7/16" pile height

One 24mm "D"-type animal nose and lock washer

Three 1-7/8" joint sets for the legs and head

Two 1-3/4" joint sets for the arms

One 2-3/8" growler (optional)

In addition, for both sizes:

Small piece of black knit suede to cover nose

Two 12mm animal eyes and lock washers

Black perle cotton No. 3—thick

Nylon stocking to cover growler (optional)

Polyester fiberfill

Artist acrylic paint for tinting fur (see page 105)

1 yd grosgrain or picot-edged ribbon, 1" wide

Pattern Pieces:

Make a full set of 11 pattern templates from the patterns on pages 144 to 147 for the small size, or pages 138 to 143 for the large size.

Cutting Directions: *Follow the two fur layout diagrams, one for each size.*

Cut four Ears and four Arms. Cut two each of Leg Front, Leg Back, and Head Back. Cut one each of Face, Body Front, Body Back, Body Left Side, and Body Right Side. There are 19 fur pieces. On the wrongside, transfer all pattern markings.

Trimming the Pile:

From the rightside, holding scissors flat against the backing, trim the pile from all 1/4" seam allowances.

Finishing the Edges:

If your fur ravels, finish the pieces along the opening edges. (See Chapter 6.)

First Pinning:

1. Pin two Ear pieces together along the curved edges, leaving bottom edges open. Repeat for the other ear. (Fig. 11.2)

2. Pin two Arm pieces together, matching dots, leaving open where indicated for stuffing. Repeat for the other arm. (Fig. 11.3)

3. Pin the Head Backs together along the center back seam, leaving open between dots. (Fig. 11.4)

4. Pin the Body Front to the Body Right Side, matching single notches. (Fig. 11.5)

5. Pin the Body Back to the Body Left Side, leaving open between dots. (Fig. 11.6)

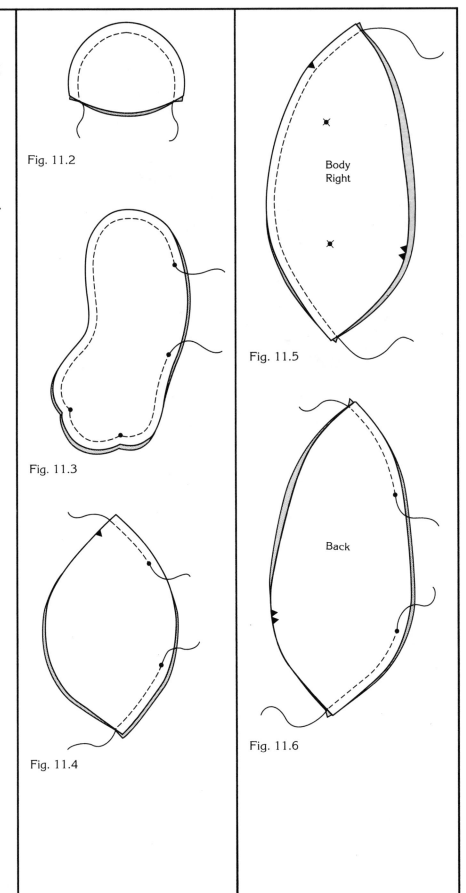

Fig. 11.2

Fig. 11.3

Fig. 11.4

Body Right

Fig. 11.5

Back

Fig. 11.6

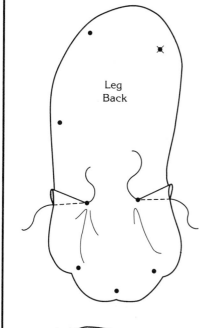

Leg
Back

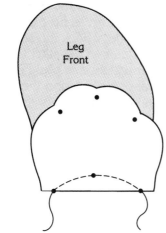

Leg
Front

Fig. 11.7

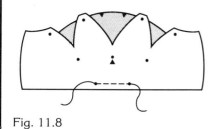

Fig. 11.8

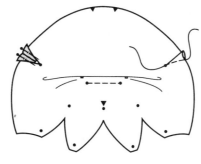

Fig. 11.9

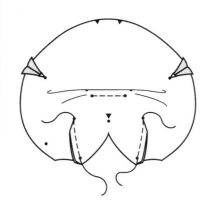

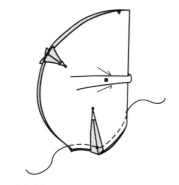

Fig. 11.10

First Stitching: *All seam allowances are 1/4".*

1. Stitch two Ear pieces along the curved edges, leaving the bottom open. Repeat for other ear. (Fig. 11.2)

2. Sew two Arm pieces together, leaving open where marked. Pivot the stitching at the dots between the fingers. Repeat for other arm. (Fig. 11.3)

3. Stitch the center back seam of the head, leaving open between the dots. (Fig. 11.4)

4. Seam the Body Front to the Body Right Side. (Fig. 11.5)

5. Seam the Body Back to the Body Left Side, leaving open between dots. (Fig. 11.6)

6. For the heels, make two darts on each Leg Back. At the ankles, make one dart on each Leg Front. (Fig. 11.7)

7. Fold the Face along the solid horizontal line, matching the dots beside the eyes. Roll the fur between your fingers to prevent trapping excess pile; pin. Stitch along the broken lines from dot to dot, backstitching at both ends. This forms a tuck at the bridge of the nose. (Fig. 11.8)

8. Make two small darts at the top of the Face. Slit darts and pin open. (Fig. 11.9)

9. Make the two side darts at the bottom of the Face by matching the raw edges and stitching from the points to the center front edges. Pin darts open. After stitching these darts, pin the center front seam, matching the raw edges and the stitching lines of the two outer darts. Stitch from the dot slightly below the nose to the neck edge. (Fig. 11.10)

Eyes and Nose:

Both the large and the small Chubby Cubby take the same eyes, but the nose sizes differ. Cover the appropriate nose, and install the nose and eyes at the marked locations.

Second Pinning:

1. Pin the two halves of the body together, around the entire seam, matching notches. Align the tops and bottoms of both pieces. (Fig. 11.11)

2. Pin a Leg Front to the corresponding Leg Back, leaving open between the dots. Pin the darts on the Leg Back up. Repeat for the other leg. (Fig. 11.12)

3. Pin the Face to the Head Backs around the entire seam, matching notches. Ease the Face to fit along the cheeks, below the small darts. (Fig. 11.13)

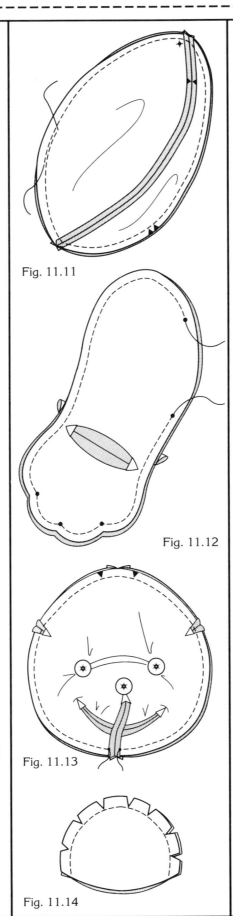

Fig. 11.11

Fig. 11.12

Fig. 11.13

Fig. 11.14

Second Stitching:

1. Sew the body pieces together in one continuous seam. (Fig. 11.11)

2. Seam the legs, leaving an opening in each for turning. (Fig. 11.12)

3. Seam the Face to the Head Backs. Begin your stitching 1/8" to the side of the center bottom seams of the head, and end it 1/8" before you reach the center bottom again. This leaves a 1/4" gap in the stitching for the neck joint. (Fig. 11.13)

Turning the Pieces:

Clip the curves of the ears. (Fig. 11.4) Turn all fur pieces to the rightside. Check the seams to make certain the stitching has not caught any pile. Free any trapped pile, using the tip of a large needle.

Jointing the Head:

Install the neck joint according to the directions in Chapter 6.

Stuffing the Head:

Since the face began as one flat piece of fabric, fiberfill must be crammed into the nose and muzzle areas in order to achieve the proper profile. This shaping takes some force; you can't accomplish it gently. The area around the darts on either side below the nose must be very firmly stuffed to support the mouth sculpting.

Working from the back head opening, first press fiberfill into the muzzle area. Try to extend the nose forward as far as possible. Fill out the forehead and cheek areas to help hold the muzzle fiberfill in place.

Next, with the first finger and thumb of one hand, press the two eyes in as you pack additional fiberfill into the nose area, pressing the nose out from the inside with your stuffing tool. Your two hands work against each other, one pushing in, the other pushing out, shaping the bridge of the nose. (Check the profile in Fig. 11.15.)

Fig. 11.15

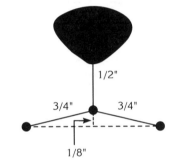
Fig. 11.16

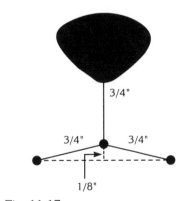
Fig. 11.17

Once the muzzle area feels solid, finish stuffing the cheeks and forehead. Although the cheeks should be nicely rounded, the center area of the muzzle should extend out further than the cheeks. Add stuffing to the center top of the head to make the face somewhat triangular, with the top narrow and the cheeks wider.

Complete stuffing by rounding the back of the head, making head's lower half wider and fuller than the top.

Sculpting the Face:

1. Mark the mouth with pins corresponding to Fig. 11.16 for the small Chubby Cubby, or Fig. 11.17 for the large size.

2. Thread a 5" soft-sculpture needle with a long, doubled length (44") of upholstery thread. Make a giant knot at the ends. Consulting Fig. 11.18, insert your needle through the back head opening, and bring it up at the pin at point 1. Remove this pin. Yank on the thread to imbed your knot in the fiberfill. Take a small stitch at point 1 to lock your thread. See Fig. 11.18.

3. Insert your needle at point 2 and come out at point 3, catching the resulting loop of thread as in Fig. 11.19. Notice that the lines of the mouth are rounded. Begin to sculpt the mouth by pulling on your thread, forming the rounded shapes for the upper lip. If necessary, coax extra fiberfill into the areas above your thread with the tip of your needle (Fig. 11.20).

4. Keeping tension on the thread, insert the needle at point 4; come up at point 1. Pull the thread taut, and once again take a small stitch at point 1 to lock your thread.

5. Insert your needle next to point 1 and bring it out at the inside corner of the eye (point 5).

6. Insert the needle close to the eye, taking a stitch about 1/8" long. Bring the needle out at point 1 again. Start sinking the eye by pushing down on it with your thumb while you pull on the thread. The corner of the mouth will turn up.

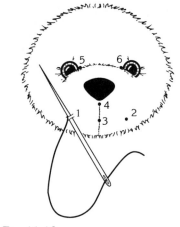

Fig. 11.18

Fig. 11.19

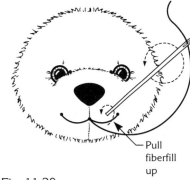

— Pull fiberfill up

Fig. 11.20

7. Insert the needle 1/8" away from point 1 and bring it out at the inside corner of the other eye (point 6). Insert the needle 1/8" away, and bring it out at point 2. Sink the second eye by pushing down on it as you pull on the thread.

8. Try to keep both eyes even, and the corners of the mouth equally turned up for Cubby's smile. Pull on the thread throughout the soft sculpting. Push down on the eyes and mold and shape the fiberfill for a cute expression.

9. Insert the needle next to point 2 and emerge at point 6. Take a stitch and come out at point 2. Take a stitch and emerge at point 5. Take a stitch and bring up your thread at point 1.

10. When you are happy with the expression, knot your thread at point 1 by taking a small stitch and passing your working thread under it and tightening. Insert your needle next to this knot and bring it out through the back head opening. Cut the thread *at the eye of the needle.* Make several surgeon's knots with the two thread ends, knotting them tightly. If you trap polyester fibers in the knot, so much the better. It securely anchors the knot. Cut the threads several inches from the knot and tuck the ends inside.

Embroidering the Mouth:

1. Thread a 7" needle with a single length of perle cotton. Make a knot 6" from the end.

2. Poke the needle through the back head opening, emerging at point 2.

3. Insert the needle at point 1. Emerge at point 3, catching your thread as in Fig. 11.19.

4. Insert your needle at point 4, coming out through the back head opening.

5. Knot your working thread snugly to your beginning 6" tail. Clip the perle cotton several inches from the knot and tuck the ends inside.

Closing the Head Opening:

With a doubled length of heavy-duty thread in a 3-1/2" needle, close the back head opening with a hidden ladder stitch.

Trimming the Muzzle:

Chubby Cubby will be cuter if you shorten the pile in the muzzle area. (Note that the cheeks, chin, and forehead are not trimmed.) Starting above the nose, shorten the pile to about half its original height. As you work up to the tuck at the bridge of the nose, shorten the pile even more, but don't trim it

Fig. 11.21

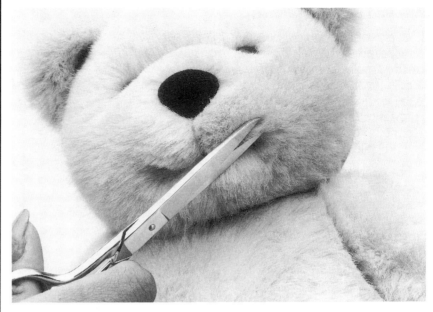

Fig. 11.22

too short or the woven backing will show through the pile.

Gradually make the pile longer toward the cheeks. When trimming below the eyes, strive for crescent-shaped, smiling eyes (Fig. 11.21). Snip off any hairs that cover the tops of the eyes.

Clip the pile at the corners of the smile and along the mouth lines so that the perle cotton shows (Fig. 11.22). Shorten the pile along the center front seam, between the nose and the mouth, to emphasize the mouth shaping. Finally, trim off any guard hairs for the entire muzzle, so that the pile is a nice, smooth plush in this area.

Jointing the Arms and Legs:

Install the joints according to the directions starting on page 68. Note that all joints for the

small Chubby Cubby are the same size, while the big Cubby has one size of joints for the arms and larger ones for the legs. (Check the materials list.)

Stuffing the Arms and Legs:

Pack fiberfill into the finger and toe curves first, keeping the seam lines smooth and even. Round out each individual finger and toe. When you fill out the foot, bend the leg at the ankle and pack extra fiberfill to define the heel shape. Next, solidly stuff the areas around the joint disks. Finish by stuffing the remainder of each arm and leg firmly.

Close the openings of the arms and legs with a hidden ladder stitch.

Paw Pad Sculpting (Arms):

1. Use a long, doubled, heavy-duty thread and a 3-1/2" needle for the small Cubby, or a 5" needle for the large Cubby. Make a knot 6" from the end. Throughout the soft sculpting, use the tip of your needle to free any pile trapped by threads.

2. For each arm, place pins corresponding to Fig. 11.23, which illustrates the outside of the right arm. The left arm will be reversed.

3. Insert the needle at the bottom seam line of the wrist (point 1). Going straight through the arm, draw the thread out at point 2. (Your 6" thread ends will dangle from point 1.)

4. Insert your needle at point 1 again, come up at point 2, and loop your thread around the outside of the arm at the wrist (Fig. 11.24). Tighten this loop and free any trapped pile. These threads must be tight; the hand shape should bulge.

5. To reinforce the first loop, form another loop on top of it: insert the needle at point 1, but this time bring it out at point 3. Tighten the threads.

6. Insert your needle on the palm side of the hand, directly below point 3. Bring your thread straight up through the hand to point 3. This makes a loop of thread around the end of the hand, between the center two fingers (Fig. 11.25). Tighten this loop.

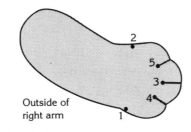

Outside of right arm

Fig. 11.23

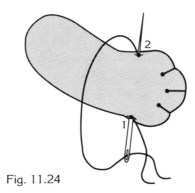

Fig. 11.24

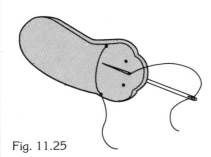

Fig. 11.25

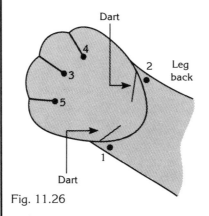

Fig. 11.26

7. For reinforcement, make another loop by inserting your needle on the palm side, directly below point 3 as before. This time, bring the needle up at point 4. Pull on the threads to tighten.

8. Similar to the loops separating the middle two fingers at point 3, make two loops of thread at point 4, and then at point 5, tightening after each stitch. End by bringing your thread up at point 1, beside your 6" ends.

9. Knot your working thread to the 6" thread ends. Lose your working thread inside the arm. Then thread the 6" ends and lose them inside also.

Foot Pad Sculpting:

Following Fig. 11.26, sculpt the toes the same as the fingers. The ankle points 1 and 2 are slightly above the base of the heel darts. The thread will loop around the back of the leg, above the heel; this roughly corresponds to the Achilles' tendon. (Don't loop the thread around the leg front.)

Finish Stuffing:

Cover the growler if appropriate.

Stuff the body firmly, packing extra fiberfill around the joints and in the neck and shoulder area. Review the information on placement of growlers on page 71. Insert the growler when you have partially completed stuffing, and finish the body.

Check how your bear sits. Chubby Cubby was designed to lean back so that he will look up at you. That way, you see his smile. If, however, your bear leans back too far, force more stuffing into the bottom of the body. You may also find it helpful to reposition the legs by rotating the outer side of the legs up with your fingers while pushing down on the joints with your thumb.

Close the body opening with a hidden ladder stitch.

Trimming Details:

1. To form a depression in the ear front, trim the pile to half its height in the area inside the pattern's dotted line.

2. On the *inside* arms only, following Fig. 11.27, shorten the pile in the center of each finger, and in a crescent shape for the palm.

3. On the *bottom* of each foot, shorten the pile as shown in Fig. 11.28 for the toes and the ball of the foot.

Tinting the Fur:

Temporarily stuff the center of each ear with a tissue to prevent the paint from bleeding through to the ear back.

Following the directions in Chapter 9, paint a scrap piece of fur to preview the color. Adjust your paint solution as necessary. When satisfied with the results of your test, tint the clipped pile in the center of each ear, the fingers, the palms, the toes, and the balls of the feet. Let dry; brush.

Fig. 11.27

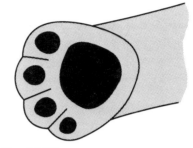

Fig. 11.28

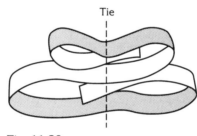

Tie

Fig. 11.29

Back of bow

Fig. 11.30

Attaching the Ears:

Finish, position, and sew the ears according to the directions for Fidget's ears, page 30.

Flat Double Bow:

This child-safe bow requires 33" of grosgrain or picot-edged ribbon about 1" wide.

1. Measure and cut 20" of ribbon. Loop it as in Fig.11.29. (A clothespin or paper clip will temporarily hold it in place.)

2. Tightly wind heavy-duty thread or dental tape (wide dental floss) around the center of the bow several times, gathering it. Knot the thread with a surgeon's square knot (page 17).

3. Fold the extra 13" length of ribbon in half, lengthwise, and tie it around the center of your loops. Use a single knot at the back of the bow (Fig. 11.30). As you tighten the ends, pull them both down to hang evenly below the loops. The 13" ribbon will only stay folded lengthwise where it has been tied. It will open up flat at the free ends.

4. Notch each end of the ribbon in an inverted "V."

5. With doubled upholstery thread, securely sew the bow to the top of the bear's back, close to his neck.

Accessories:

Chubby Cubby has many talents. He can play with his own set of stuffed blocks (directions follow) or he can hold a Cat's Cradle. No other teddies can make such a claim.

The Cat's Cradle for the large Chubby Cubby requires about 60" of decorative cord, such as rattail. Or make your own cord with embroidery floss. (See Fig. 7.26.)

The easiest way to wind the cord on Chubby's paws is to construct the Cat's Cradle on him the same way you would on yourself. Following the soft-sculpting diagram (Fig. 11.23), place a pin at points 3 and 5 on both paws. Wrap the cord around his wrists and around these pins on his second fingers. Check the color photo to confirm that you have it right.

When the entire Cat's Cradle is snug, knot the ends of the cord at the bottom of one wrist. With upholstery thread and a 3-1/2" needle, tack the cord to both arms at points 1, 2, 3, and 5 (as in Fig. 11.23). Remove the pins.

If, over time, the Cat's Cradle loosens, tighten it by pulling your bear's paws apart from each other.

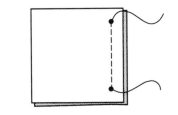

Fig. 11.31

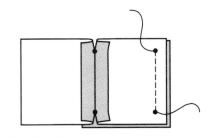

Fig. 11.32

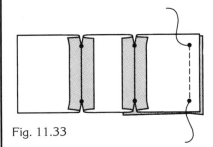

Fig. 11.33

Chubby Blocks

Finished sizes: 1-3/4" square or 2" square

The right accessory sets off a teddy bear to perfection, like Chubby Cubby and these stuffed blocks. Both come in two sizes. (The embroidery is the same for either.)

These blocks coordinate with the quilts in Chapter 8. You have a choice of three blocks with C-U-B lettering or with Beary, Merry, and Holly Days (page 138), with the words "Holly Days" combined on one block. The B-E-A-R charts (page 98) could also be used for a different set of four blocks.

Check Chapter 4 for general cross stitch directions. In addition, Chapter 8 explains the French knot for the Beary Merry Holly Days chart.

Materials:

Three finished C-U-B designs, each letter worked on an individual 4" square of 11 count white Aida (or three finished "Beary Merry Holly Days" designs, each worked on an individual 4" square of 14 count white Aida)

Extra Aida for the back of each block

Remnants of four or more coordinating print fabrics (100% cotton recommended). You will need enough material to cut a total of twelve pattern squares.

Polyester fiberfill

Cutting Directions:

Select either the small or the large block pattern on page 138. Cut a total of 12 pattern pieces from your various print fabrics.

Carefully trim the three completed Aida squares to the size of the selected pattern piece, keeping the designs centered.

Cut three additional pattern pieces from the extra Aida.

Block Assembly: *All seam allowances are 1/4". Finger press seams open after stitching.*

Note: the directions are written for one block. If you repeat each step three times, however, you'll make all three blocks at the same time.

1. With rightsides together, seam two fabric squares along one side, from dot to dot. See Fig. 11.31.

2. With rightsides together, seam another fabric square to the opposite side of the second square, from dot to dot (Fig. 11.32).

3. With rightsides together, seam the fourth fabric square to the opposite side of the third square, from dot to dot (Fig. 11.33).

4. Align the top edge of the first fabric square with the bottom edge of one of your embroidered Aida squares. Start machine stitching at the dot, with the Aida toward the feed dogs. Stitch across the bottom of the Aida square, leaving the needle in the material

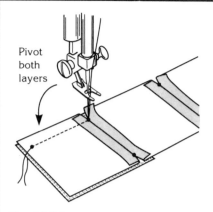

Pivot both layers

Fig. 11.34

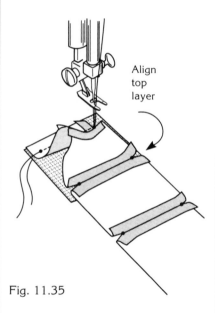

Align top layer

Fig. 11.35

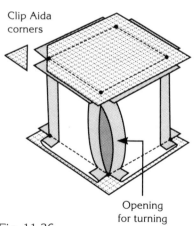

Clip Aida corners

Opening for turning

Fig. 11.36

when you reach the second dot (at the beginning of the second fabric square). Lift your presser foot and pivot the Aida 90° to align the second side for sewing (Fig.11.34). Pull the free end of the print fabrics toward you to match the edge of the second fabric with the next side of the Aida square. See Fig. 11.35.

5. Stitch the second side of the Aida square, once again stopping the stitching at the dot and pivoting. Align and stitch the third and fourth fabrics to the remaining sides of the Aida square. Your stitching should meet at the beginning dot.

6. Likewise, attach the plain Aida square to the back of the cube (Fig. 11.36).

7. Trim the corners of the Aida squares. Turn the block to the rightside through the opening between the first and fourth print fabrics. Turning the small block is tricky. To start it, push an opposite corner gently through the opening with the handle of a wooden spoon.

8. Firmly stuff the block, watching the corners. The fiberfill tends to pack in the middle, so coax extra into each corner. You'll notice from the photos that the finished shape is somewhat rounded, giving a soft appearance, but make sure you end up with a block, not a ball.

9. Turn the raw edges under 1/4" and slip stitch the opening closed. Hide the thread ends inside.

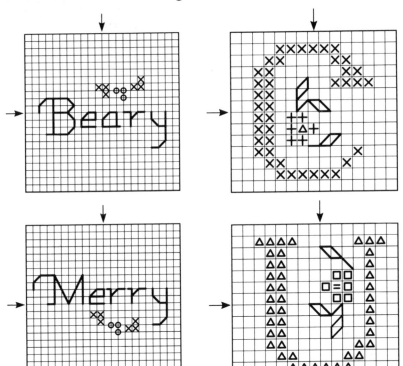

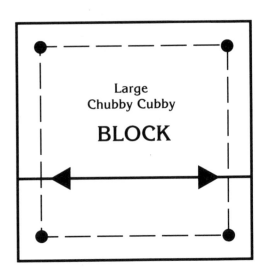

Large
Chubby Cubby

BLOCK

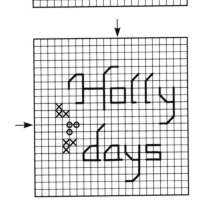

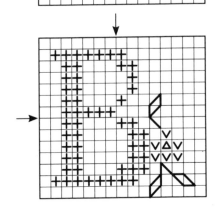

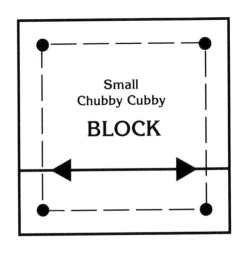

Small
Chubby Cubby

BLOCK

KEY   **DMC COLOR NUMBER:**

XX	699 Christmas Green
⊙⊙	666 Christmas Red, bright (French knot)
⌐	Outline: 321 Christmas Red

KEY   **DMC COLOR NUMBER:**

XX	519 Sky Blue
△△	743 Yellow
□□	353 Peach
==	351 Dk. Coral
VV	210 Lavender
++	776 Pink
╱	Outline: 564 Lt. Green

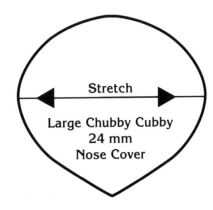

Stretch

Large Chubby Cubby
24 mm
Nose Cover

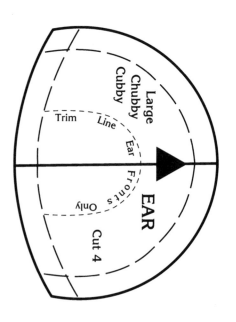

Large
Chubby
Cubby

Trim Line

Ear
Fronts
Only

Cut 4

EAR

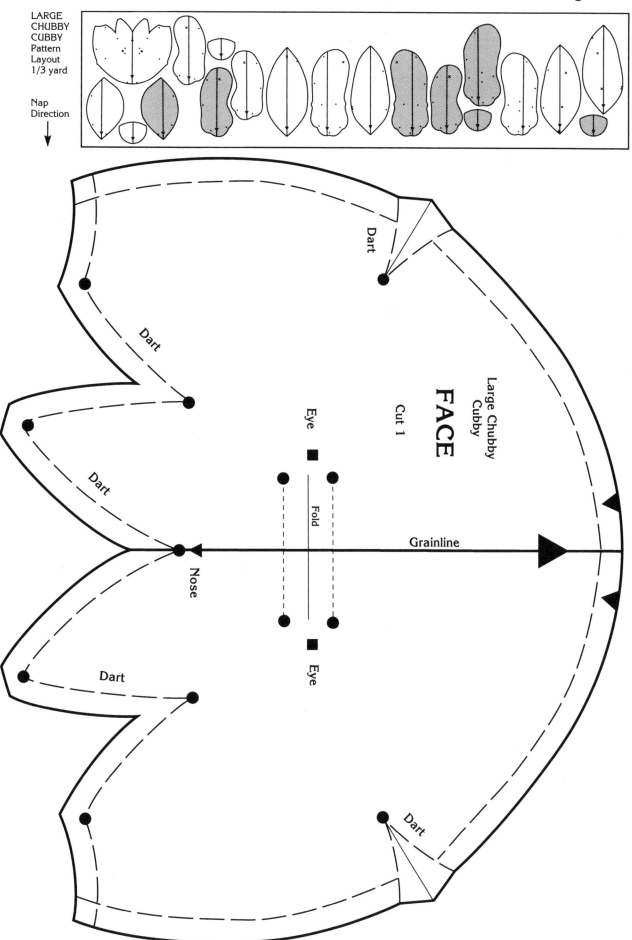

LARGE
CHUBBY
CUBBY
Pattern
Layout
1/3 yard

Nap
Direction

Dart

Dart

Dart

Nose

Dart

Eye

Fold

Eye

Grainline

Large Chubby
Cubby

FACE

Cut 1

Dart

Dart

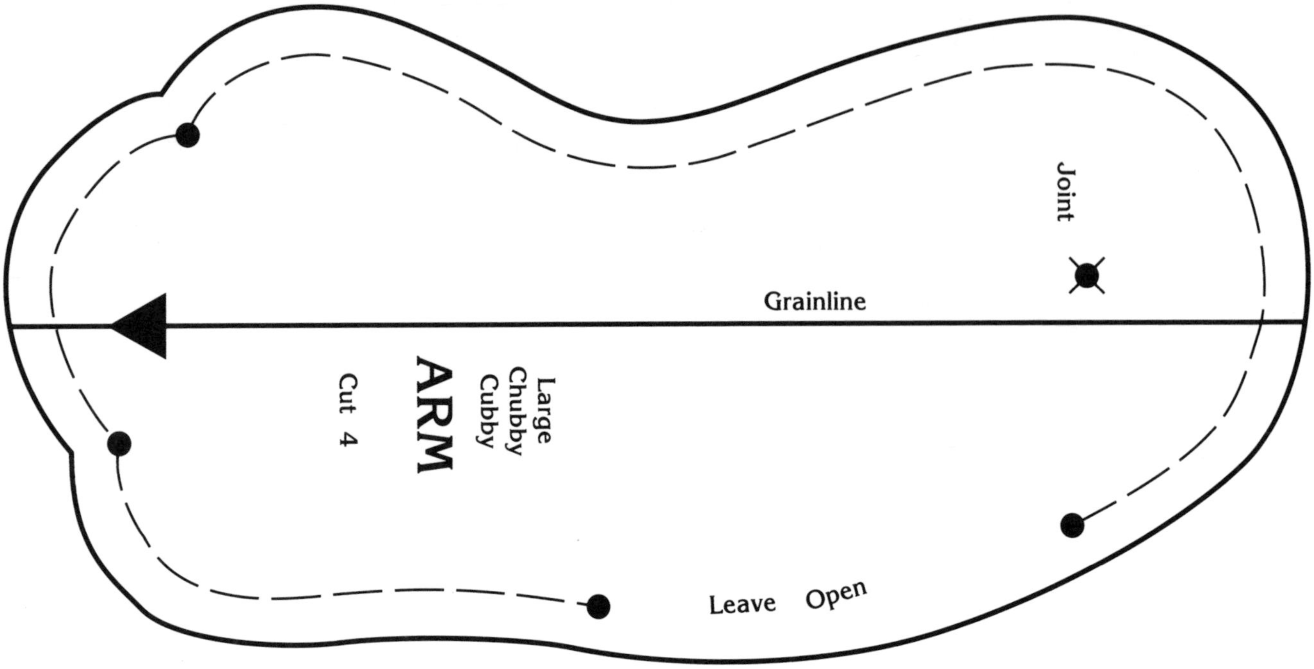

Joint

Grainline

Large
Chubby
Cubby

ARM

Cut 4

Leave Open

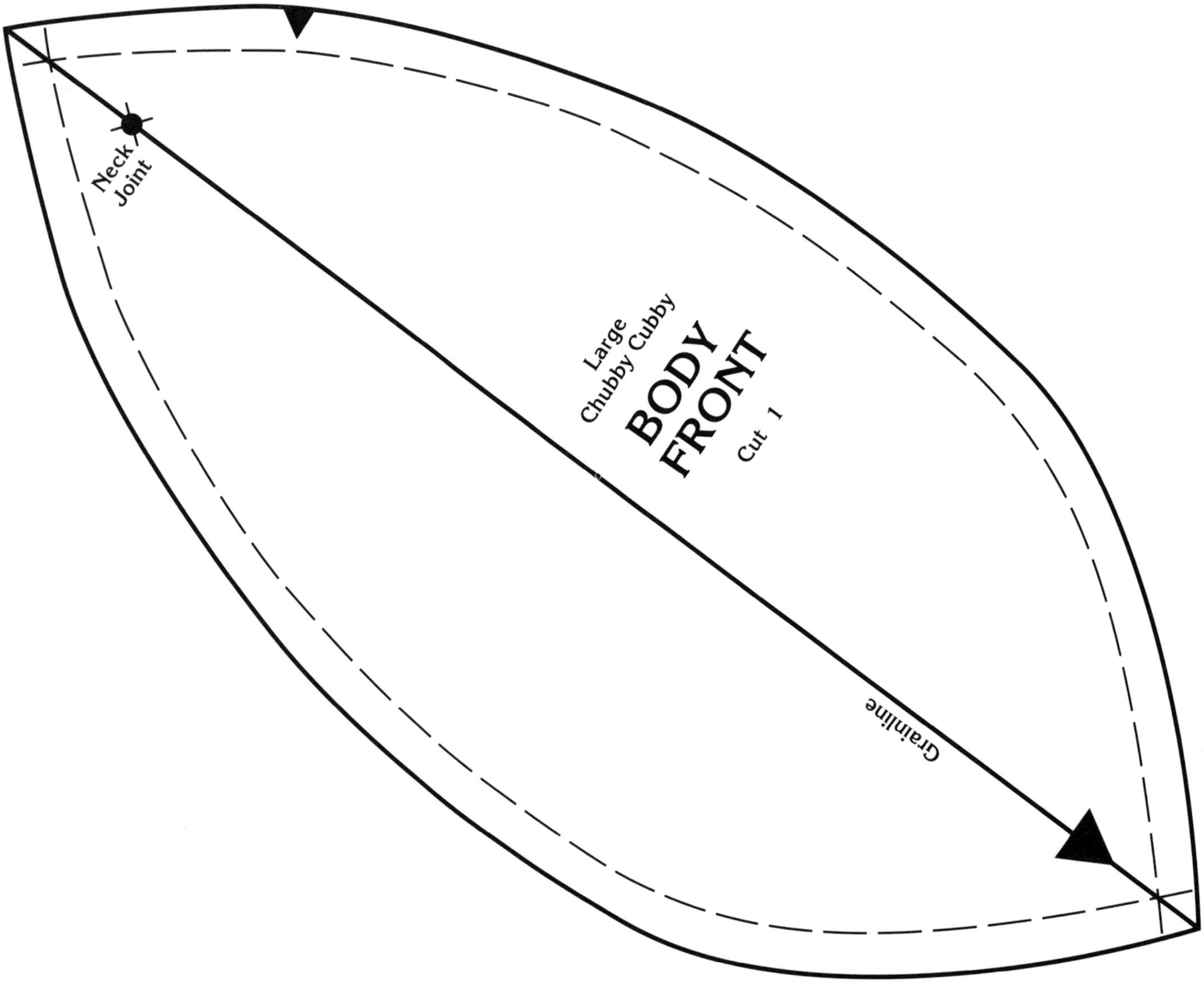

Neck
Joint

Large
Chubby Cubby

**BODY
FRONT**

Cut 1

Grainline

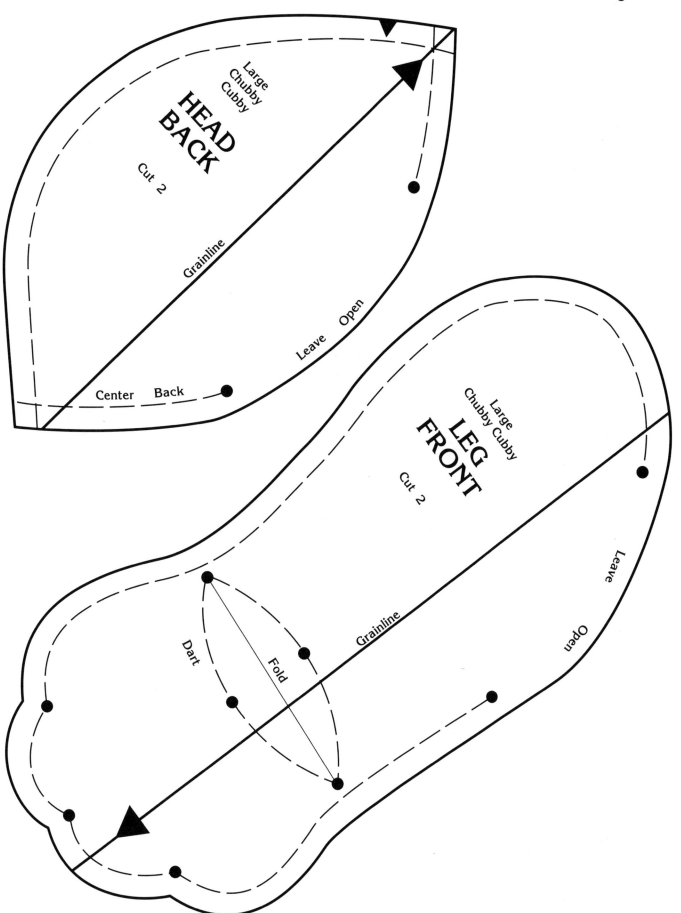

Large
Chubby
Cubby

**HEAD
BACK**

Cut 2

Grainline

Leave   Open

Center   Back

Large
Chubby Cubby

**LEG
FRONT**

Cut 2

Leave

Open

Grainline

Dart

Fold

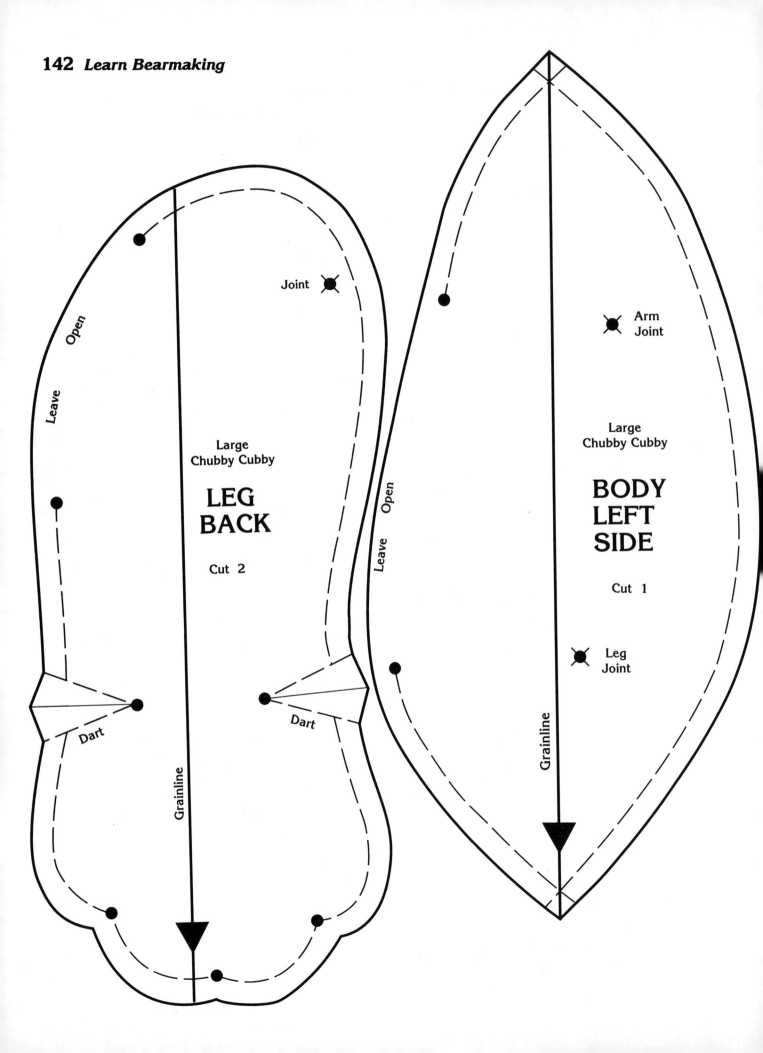

Leave Open

Joint

Leave Open

Large
Chubby Cubby

LEG
BACK

Cut 2

Dart

Dart

Grainline

Arm
Joint

Large
Chubby Cubby

BODY
LEFT
SIDE

Cut 1

Leg
Joint

Grainline

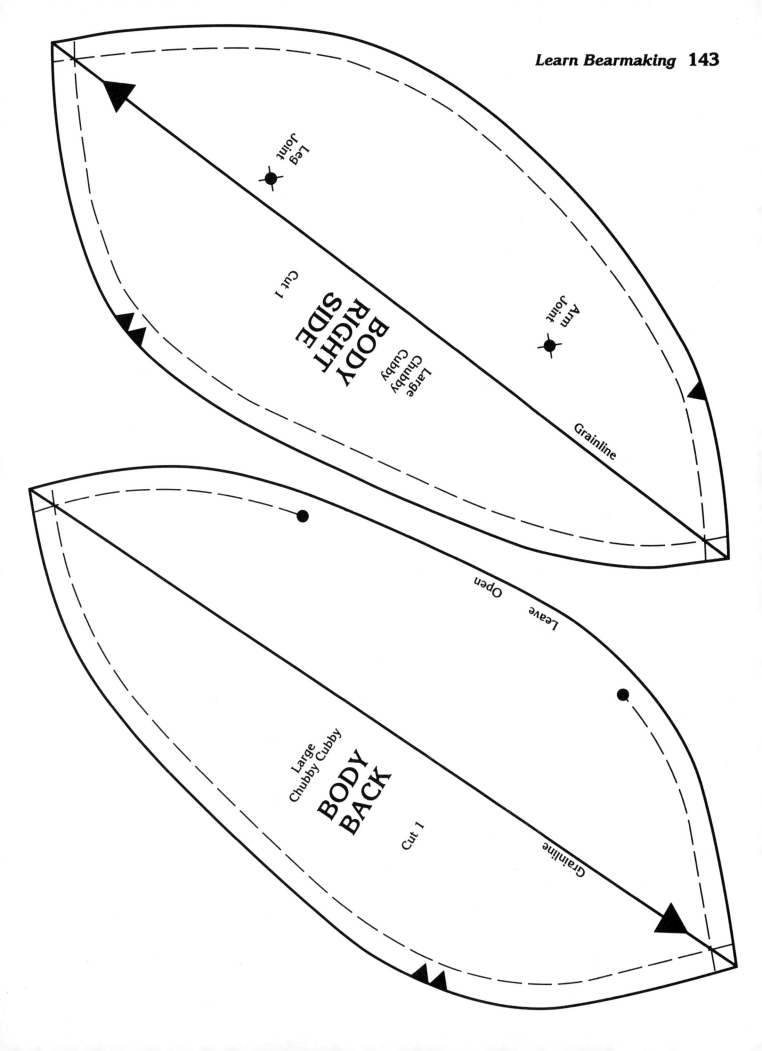

BODY RIGHT SIDE
Cut 1
Large Chubby Cubby
Leg Joint
Arm Joint
Grainline

BODY BACK
Large Chubby Cubby
Cut 1
Leave Open
Grainline

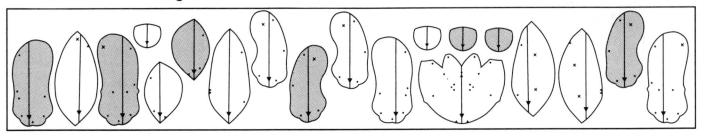

Small Chubby Cubby
Pattern Layout
1/4 yd

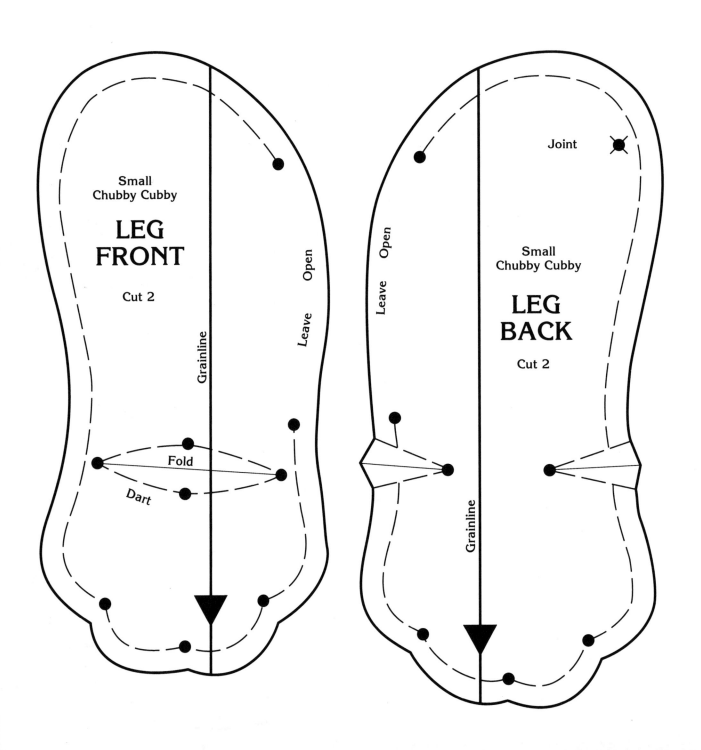

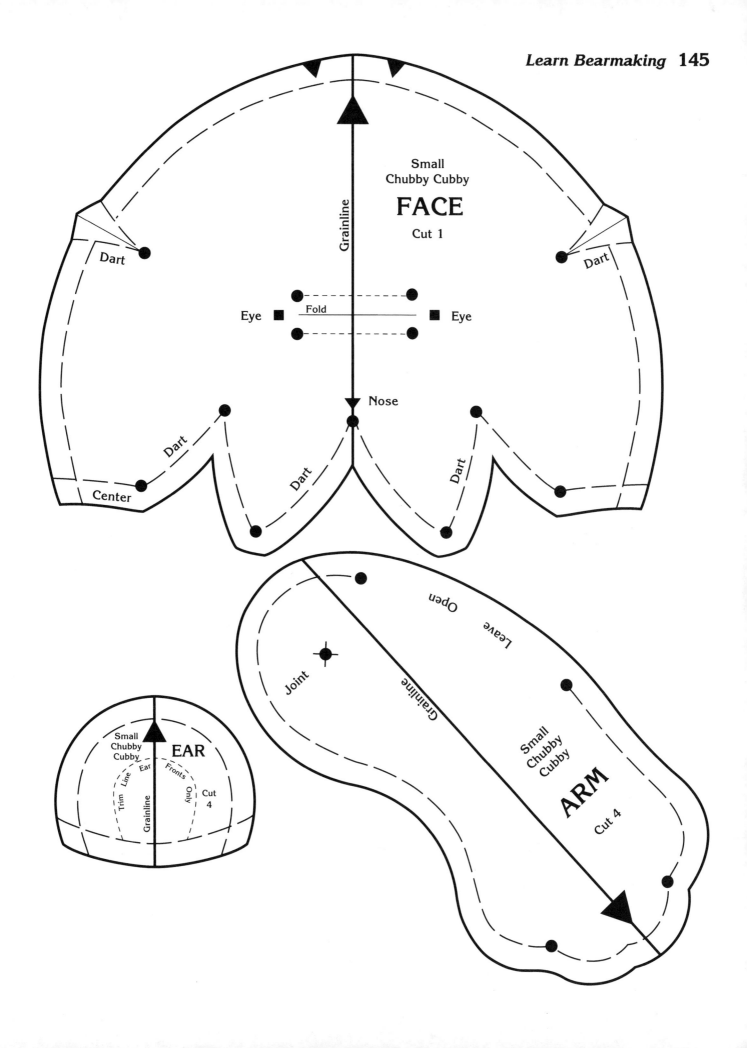

Small
Chubby Cubby
FACE
Cut 1

Grainline

Dart

Dart

Eye ■ Fold ■ Eye

Nose

Dart Dart Dart Dart

Center

Small
Chubby
Cubby

EAR

Small
Chubby
Cubby
Ear
Fronts
Only
Cut
4
Trim Line
Grainline

Joint

Leave Open

Grainline

Small
Chubby
Cubby

ARM

Cut 4

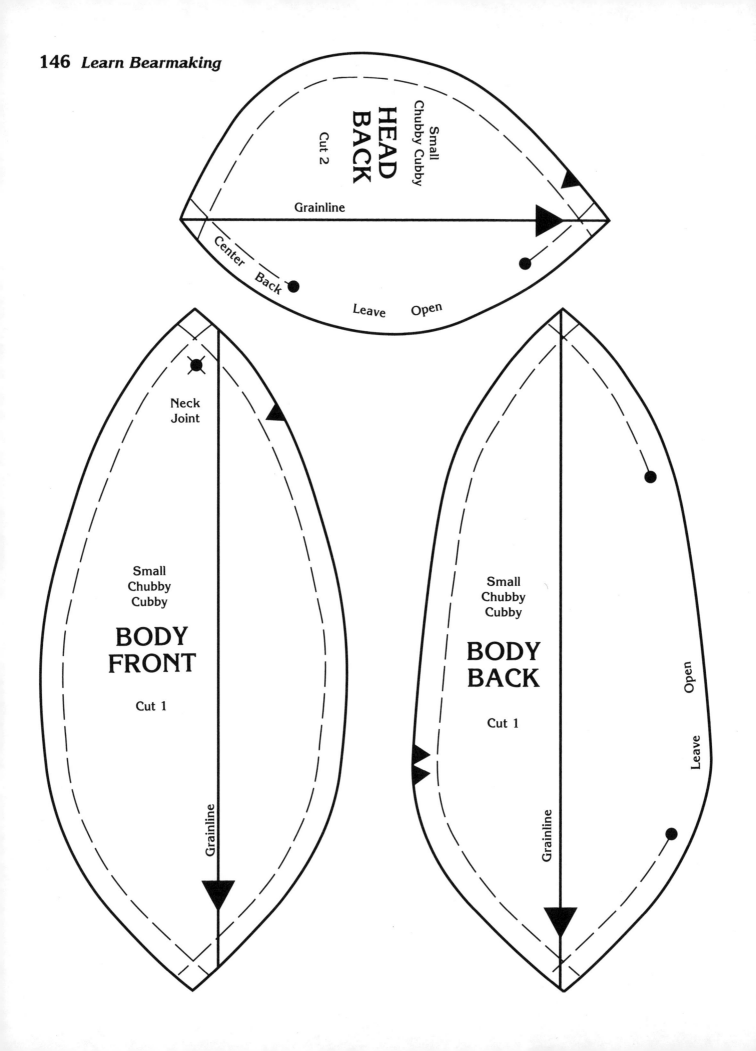

Small
Chubby Cubby

**HEAD
BACK**

Cut 2

Grainline

Center Back

Leave   Open

Neck
Joint

Small
Chubby
Cubby

**BODY
FRONT**

Cut 1

Grainline

Small
Chubby
Cubby

**BODY
BACK**

Cut 1

Leave   Open

Grainline

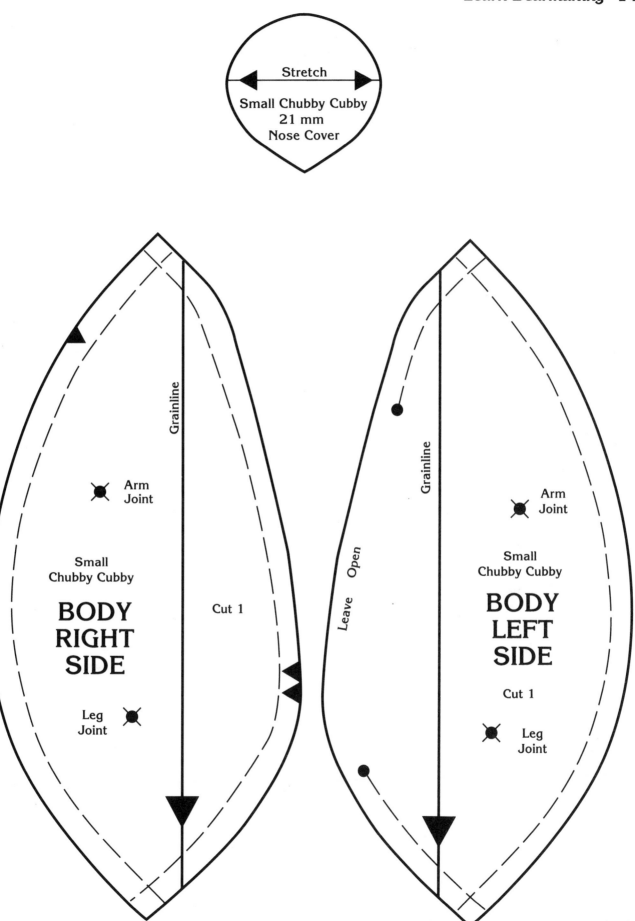

Stretch

Small Chubby Cubby
21 mm
Nose Cover

Grainline

Arm
Joint

Small
Chubby Cubby

**BODY
RIGHT
SIDE**

Cut 1

Leg
Joint

Leave Open

Grainline

Arm
Joint

Small
Chubby Cubby

**BODY
LEFT
SIDE**

Cut 1

Leg
Joint

12. Insbearation

Conclusion

Throughout the text, you may have noticed references to "teddy bear artists." I've delayed discussing the term until now for a reason. Teddy bear artists make original teddy bears, in many more media than fur—i.e., painting, silver, gold, wood, clay, etc. If teddy bear artists work in fabric, that means they design each pattern piece on their own. Most of them work in mohair, a luxurious, if costly, fabric. Because every part of the teddy bear comes from within the individual, every original artist bear is unique.

There are thousands of teddy bear collectors. Some collect all kinds of bearaphernalia, while others focus exclusively on original artist bears. The main attraction is the diversity and the individuality of each artist's bears' faces.

I didn't explain "teddy bear artists" earlier, because I wanted you to gain confidence by making tested patterns. If you now wish to design your own bears, start by trial and error. Work on one piece at a time, drawing it freehand, sewing it up, revising the shape, and sewing it again until it's exactly what you had in mind. Experiment with different fabrics and textures. As the designer, you are free to make your bear whatever way suits you. And because your bear comes from inside you, he will speak to you in a way no manufactured bear ever could.

I'd like nothing better than for my designs and the designs of my peers to inspire new teddy bear artists. Join us. The field needs your ideas and energy.

Regardless of whether you design originals or use patterns, you touch the future when you give one of your handmade teddies to a special someone. Your creation will thrive long after he has left your hands—because a teddy's life begins when he has found someone to love.

To illustrate this point, let me tell you about a friend's experience in a teddy bear restoration service. She once worked on a bear nearly 80 years old. He was in terrible shape. The family dog had chewed his face. The bear's terminally ill owner lay in a convalescent home, and the lady's granddaughter had brought this mangled teddy bear to my friend for repairs. The restorer worked from an old photograph that showed the bear brand-new, with his owner, then only three years old. Painstakingly, the artist rewove the missing fabric of the bear's face, thread by thread, and matched and patched the pile one tuft of fiber at a time. When completed, she had reconstructed the bear to his original appearance.

The granddaughter brought the bear to her grandmother. The entire family gathered at her bedside. They didn't expect a reaction from her, but they gently laid that teddy bear in her arms anyway. At the touch of the familiar fur, the grandmother opened her eyes. Tears rolled down her cheeks when she realized it was her childhood bear. In a frail voice, she told her family not to worry about her, that she was content, and now that she had her best friend from childhood, she could die in peace. Later, the teddy bear was buried with her, together forever.

That story pulls at my heartstrings. No other stuffed animal or doll, no other gift, no matter what price, would have had the same impact and power as that simple teddy bear. Do you think an unknown bearmaker could have imagined, in the early 1900's, what an important role his or her teddy would play in that grandmother's life?

In the same way, contemporary bearmakers can't begin to fathom the destinies of all the bears they create. But every teddy bear knows. Inside his heart he yearns to be that one special bear to someone—to form a perfect bond with one child, or with one adult who has not lost contact with the child within.

Give your teddy a chance to be that special bear. Now that you've learned bearmaking, why not practice beargiving.

Glossary

Aida: An evenweave fabric for use in counted cross stitch embroidery. The most common sizes are 11, 14, or 18 squares to the inch.

Backstitch: Fig. 4.33.

Block: Place finished counted cross stitched material face down on a padded surface. Smooth out any wrinkles. Cover with a damp press cloth (cotton, muslin, flour-sack dishcloth, etc.). Press with a dry iron preheated to "Wool." Place the iron down, applying gentle pressure for a few seconds. Reposition the iron by lifting instead of sliding. After pressing the entire piece, remove the press cloth. Do not raise the embroidery from the padded surface until it is completely dry.

Clip curves: Fig. 11.14.

Evenweave: Special fabric designed specifically for counted cross stitch embroidery. Its surface is divided into small squares that correspond to the charted design's grid.

Finger press: After sewing a seam, substitute finger pressure for ironing.

Grade seams: To trim one seam allowance narrower than the other, in order to reduce bulk.

Guard hairs: Sparse fibers that extend 1/8" to 1/4" above the main pile height.

Hardanger: An evenweave fabric with 22 squares to the

inch, for use in counted cross stitch embroidery.

Hidden ladder stitch: Figs. 3.13-3.15.

Layer seam: Same as "grade seam."

Overcast:

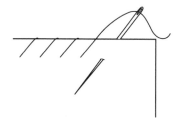

Running stitch:

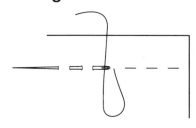

Satin stitch: Solid, parallel straight stitches, usually done on an angle.

Selvage: For woven furs, the lengthwise edge that does not ravel. For knit furs, the lengthwise edge (can be either cut or finished).

Slip stitch:

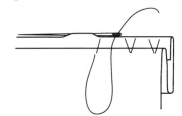

Stay stitch: A line of straight, machine stitching next to the seam line to prevent stretching. Usually done just inside the seam allowance on one layer of fabric at a time.

Teddy bear artist: See p. 148 .

Top stitch:

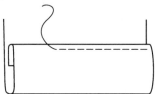

Trim seams: Reducing the width of the seam allowances by cutting them. With shears parallel to the seam line, two layers may be trimmed at once, reducing them an equal amount. Compare "grade seams," above.

Underfur: Fibers that are shorter than the main pile height. An underfur supports the main pile fibers and helps hide the fabric's backing. See Figs. 6.1 and 6.2.

Walking foot: A sewing machine attachment that feeds the top layer of fabric. Prevent uneven seams on bulky materials.

Bibiliography

Children's Teddy Bear Books Plus

Children's list prepared by Doris C. Losey, Youth Specialist, Tampa/Hillsborough County Public Library System (Florida)

Teddy bears have a long history of starring in their own books; now they star in films and videos, too. Libraries often use teddies to introduce young children to libraries and books in a welcoming way. For example, during National Library Week in April, one library gave library cards to teddies, too. The following is a list of good teddy bear books for story hour and play, at your home or at the library. (E means picture books, easy to read, and are in a separate section of the children's department. J books are shelved in the juvenile fiction section alphabetically by author's last name.)
(Publisher's note: If you've truly learned both bearmaking and beargiving, why not make a Fidget for the children's department of your local library?)

Read-to Books

E Douglass, Barbara. *Good As New*, Lothrop, 1982. Grady wonders if his teddy bear will ever be the same after his cousin drags it by the ears, tries to feed it to the dogs, and buries it. Luckily Grandpa comes to the rescue.

E Freeman, Don, *Corduroy*, Viking Press, 1968. The adventures of a teddy bear living in a department store when he searches for a missing button.

E Freeman, Don, *A Pocket for Corduroy*, Viking Press, 1978. Trying to find a pocket for his overalls, Corduroy has a series of misadventures in a laundromat.

E Gili, Phillida, *The Lost Ears*, Julia MacRae Books/Franklin Watts, 1981. Harry, a teddy bear only 2-1/2" tall, loses his ears and is rejected by his boy, Oliver, until he is rescued by Lucy, who makes him a new pair of ears, a red jacket, and a blue scarf for cold days.

J Hower, Deborah, *The Teddy Bear's Scrapbook*, Atheneum, 1980. On a rainy day, Teddy shares his scrapbook of pictures and newspaper clippings about his past as a cowboy, a reporter, and a Hollywood star.

E Kennedy, Jimmy, *The Teddy Bear's Picnic*, Green Tiger Press, 1983. Surprises occur on a teddy bear's picnic (record included).

E Ormondroyd, Edward, *Theodore*, Parnassus Press, 1966. Another bear's adventures with the laundry clean him up so much that his little girl, Lucy, doesn't recognize him until he gets help from some of his dog friends.

E Ormondroyd, Edward, *Theodore's Rival*, Parnassus Press, 1971. Theodore is jealous when Lucy receives another bear for her birthday, until he realizes that Benjamin is a panda which is not really a bear at all.

E Waber, Bernard, *Ira Sleeps Over*, Houghton Mifflin, 1972. Ira doesn't know whether to take his teddy along on his first sleep-over, because his big sister says his friend will make fun of him. But when his friend, Reggie, begins to tell ghost stores, Ira knows that he needs his teddy bear.

E Wells, Rosemary, *Peabody* Dial, 1983. Peabody is Annie's best friend until she is given Rita, a talking/singing doll. Now Peabody sits on the shelf, waiting for Annie to remember him.

Films and Videos

Corduroy, Weston Woods, 1984, 16 min., color. Live-action film about Corduroy's adventures. Also available in video.

Ira Sleeps Over, Phoenix Films, 1977, 17 min., color. Live-action film about Ira and his teddy bear, who sleep over at Reggie's house.

Pocket for Corduroy, Phoenix Films, 1986, 20 min., color. Live-action film about Corduroy's further adventures.

Fingerplays, Songs, and Games

"This is a cuddly teddy bear," from *Busy Bodies: Finger Plays and Action Rhymes*, revised edition, Marlene Gawron, Moonlight Press, 1985, p. 37.

"Teddy bear, teddy bear, turn around," from *Story Programs: A Source Book of Materials*, Carolyn Sue Peterson and Brenny Hall, Scarecrow Press, 1980, pp. 101-102—can be used as a fingerplay or a song.

"Teddy Bear Picnic Game," from *Mudluscious: Stories and Activities Featuring Food for Preschool Children*, Jan Irving and Robin Curie, Libraries Unlimited, 1986, pp. 25-26.

Classics

Bond, Michael, *A Bear Called Paddington*, Dell, 1968. (Also available in video.)

Clise, Michele Durkson, as told to Alf Collins, *My Circle of Bears*, Green Tiger Press, 1981.

Eaton, Seymour, *The Roosevelt Bears: Their Travels and Adventures*, Dover, 1979.

Milne, A.A., *Winnie-the-Pooh*, Dell, 1970. (Also available in video.)

Adult Teddy Bear Books

Bialosky, Peggy and Alan, *The TeddyBear Catalog*, Workman Publishing, 1980.

Bull, Peter, *The Teddy Bear Book*, Hobby House, 1986.

Keyes, Josa, *The Teddy Bear Story*, Multimedia Publications (U.K.), 1985.

Menten, Ted, *The TeddyBear Lovers Catalog*, Courage Books (a division of Running Press), 1985.

Menten, Ted, *Teddy's Bearzaar*, Running Press, 1988.

Schoonmaker, Patricia N., *A Collector's History of the Teddy Bear*, Hobby House, 1981.

Mullins, Linda, *Teddy Bears Past & Present*, Hobby House, 1986.

Mullins, Linda, *The Teddy Bear Men, Theodore Roosevelt and Clifford Berryman*, Hobby House, 1987.

Waugh, Carol-Lynn Rössel, *Teddy Bear Artists*, Hobby House Press, 1984.

Needlework Books

Learn How Book (Knitting, Crocheting, Tatting, Embroidery), Coats & Clark's Book No. 170-D, 1975.

De Sarigny, Rudi, *How to Make and Design Stuffed Toys*, Dover, 1971.

Fanning, Robbie and Tony, *The Complete Book of Machine Embroidery*, Chilton, 1986.

Magazines

Cross Stitch & Country Crafts, Craftways, 4118 Lakeside Drive, Richmond, CA 94806

Sew News, PO Box 1790, Peoria, IL 61656

Teddy Bear and friends, Hobby House Press, Inc., 900 Frederick Street, Cumberland, MD 21502

Teddy Bear Review, Collector Communications Corp., 170 Fifth Avenue, New York, NY 10010

The Teddy Tribune, 254 W. Sidney, St. Paul, MN 55107

Threads, The Taunton Press, Inc., Box 355, Newtown, CT 06470

Index

Suppliers

Bear Clawset
27 Palermo Walk
Long Beach, CA 90803
(213) 434-8077
Knit furs for Wispy and Bearly Adequate and more; $2 catalog

Bears in the Wood
59 N. Santa Cruz Avenue
Los Gatos, CA 95030
(408)354-6974
Artists' teddy bears

Carver's Eye Co.
P. O. Box 16692
Portland, OR 97216
(503) 666-5680
12mm and 15mm dark brown animal safety eyes (Style Nos. 40 and 50, respectively); 15mm black safety eyes (Style No. 50); triangular noses with safety washers (Style Nos. 721D and 724D); plastic joint sets; metal lock washers in bulk; $1 catalog

Clotilde
1909 S.W. First Avenue
Ft. Lauderdale, FL 33315
(305)761-8655
Plastic safety eyes, dollmaking needles, quilting supplies; $1 catalog

Delaney's Bear House
Jo Anne Delaney
7316 E. McKinley
Scottsdale, AZ 85257
(602) 947-6077
Tempered hardboard joint discs, bolts and locknuts; send LSASE.

Disco Joints
305 Bedford Rd
Kitchener, Ont N2G 3A7
Canada
Complete line of bearmaking supplies. SASE for price list; Canadian orders only.

Edinburgh Imports, Inc.
P. O. Box 722
Woodland Hills, CA 91365-0722
outside Calif: 1-(800)EDINBRG; inside Calif: (818) 703-1122
German woven synthetic furs, growlers, squeakers, fingertip wire brushes, Stuffing Sticks™, joints (fiberboard discs, bolts, locknuts)

Intercal Trading Group
P. O. Box 11337
Costa Mesa, CA 92627
(714) 645-9396
German woven synthetic furs, hardboard joint sets (machine screw and locknut), growlers

Jen-Cel-Lite Corporation
954 East Union Street
Seattle, WA 98122
Gametted Polyester Fiberfill, 20 lb. minimum

Making It
242 Kent Avenue
Kentfield, CA 94904
(415) 461-5398
EasyGrip Stuffing Sticks™ specifically for bearmaking

Nancy's Notions
P.O. Box 683
Beaver Dam, WI 53916
(414) 887-0391
Gingher shears, Quilting templates, Pioneer Thimbles™, Needle Grabbers, full line of sewing notions; free catalog

Spare Bear Parts
P.O. Box 56-M
Interlochen, MI 49643
(616)275-6993
American and Canadian knit furs, polyester fiberfill, stuffing tools, ribbon, custom printed labels; $1 fabric sample card

The Teddy Works
5-15 49th Avenue
Long Island City, NY 11101
Full range of bearmaking supplies; free catalog

WHOLESALE SUPPLIERS

Borg Textile Corporation
P. O. Box 697
105 Maple Street
Rossville, GA 30741
(404) 866-1743
Knit furs

Bunka Embroidery International
P. O. Box 10321
Charleston, SC 29411
(803) 552-0440
Bunka brushes (for fur trapped in seams)

Carver's Eye Co.
P. O. Box 16692
Portland, Oregon 97216
(503) 666-5680
12mm and 15mm dark brown animal eyes, 15mm black eyes; triangular noses with safety washers; plastic joint sets

J. L. DeBall of America, Ltd.
111 West 40th Street
New York, NY 10018
(212) 575-8613
German woven synthetics

Monterey Mills, Inc.
P. O. Box 271
1725 E. Delavan Dr.
Janesville, WI 53545
(608) 754-8309
Knit furs

Zims, Inc.
4370 South 3rd West
Salt Lake City, Utah 84107
Safety eyes, noses, plastic joints, and lamb growlers